How People Get Power

How People Get Power

Revised Edition

SI KAHN

with a foreword by
U.S. Senator Paul David Wellstone

and an introduction by
Chandra Talpade Mohanty

NASW PRESS

An NASW Press/Grassroots Leadership Book

National Association of Social Workers
Washington, DC • 1994

Ann A. Abbott, PhD, ACSW, President
Sheldon R. Goldstein, ACSW, LISW, Executive Director

Linda Beebe, Executive Editor
Nancy Winchester, Editorial Services Director
Annette Hansen, Copy Editor
Susan Harris, Proofreader
Robert Elwood, Indexer

Cover and interior design by Naylor Design, Inc.

This book was composed by Harlowe Typography, Inc., and printed by Kirby Lithographic Company, Inc.

Library of Congress Cataloging-in-Publication Data

Kahn, Si.
  How people get power / Si Kahn.—Rev. ed.
    p. cm.
  "Grassroots Leadership Book."
  Includes bibliographical references and index.
  ISBN 0-87101-236-7
  1. Community development. 2. Power (Social sciences) I. Title.
HN49.C6K34 1994
307.1′4—dc20   94-10537
                                                CIP

Dedicated
to the memory
of my mother,
Rosalind Kahn,
who believed in justice,
and of
Mervin Barr,
who believed in freedom.

They say one night Roosevelt couldn't sleep. Well, his wife asked him what was the matter, and he said, "I keep hearing the hungry children crying. You know, I ordered them to plow under all that wheat, and I can't sleep for hearing the children crying for bread." She said, "Well, why don't you put cotton in your ears?" "I can't," he said, "I had that plowed under too."

Clinton Patrick
Cob Hill, Kentucky

Whenever you have a birth, you have three things that go with it: blood, pain and water. Some folks want the birth, but they don't want to have the blood or the pain or the tears; but if you want the one, you've got to take the other with it.

Rev. Sherman Jones
Forrest City, Arkansas

Contents

Foreword

By U.S. Senator Paul David Wellstone

I first met Si Kahn in 1975. He was organizing with workers in the J. P. Stevens labor struggle, and I was writing a book about rural community organizing based on my personal experience in rural Minnesota.

Si became my teacher. Many of his brilliant insights about community organizing became the foundation for my work. I especially appreciated Si's emphasis on building leadership and his faith and confidence in people. He wasn't interested in flashy tactics; he was and is committed to empowering people to be their own leaders and to create authentic democratic politics.

How People Get Power is must reading for all of us who share this vision. It is also must reading for effective grassroots politics and progressive change in our country.

As a United States senator from Minnesota elected in 1990 with a populist–progressive campaign, I believe in the importance of electoral politics. It is one important way we contest for power in American politics. And because issues are what attract me to public service, I am very committed to good public policy. That is the essence of being a good legislator. But without grassroots organizing, electoral politics is a politics without a base. And without grassroots organizing that builds power for ordinary citizens, there is no constituency to fight for the changes in public policy in such critical areas as health care, education, and jobs.

These are perfect examples of ideas whose time has come and come and come again—each time, over the past 60 years, reform has been blocked by big-ticket interests. If what is "politically feasible" is defined by the patterns of power inside the Beltway, then once again we will fail in Congress to pass significant reform. Only with grassroots politics and pressure, based on effective community organizing, will we win these historic struggles for health care, education, and jobs.

How People Get Power is essential reading that connects with the most important question of our time: how to enable ordinary citizens to be fully participant members in a democratic society.

Preface to the First Edition

This is a book about community organizing, written for organizers. Most of the material in the book came out of my own experiences as an organizer in the rural South. If I have learned anything in that time, it is that there are really no rules for organizers—only experiences. I hope that this book will be read in that light, as the guide to one person's experience, and that other organizers will treat it as a scratching post for their own ideas.

If the examples described here seem to refer mostly to the rural South, it is because that is where I have lived and worked. I hope that many of these examples will also be useful in other rural areas of the country and in the cities, but the people who read and use this book will have to be the judges of that.

It might be helpful to add a few words concerning what this book is *not* about. It is not in any sense a history of organizing, of the civil rights movement, or of poverty in America. It is not a handbook for those who believe that this society is about to move forward together or for those who want to do something *for* poor people. It is not for those who believe that the federal government and private industry, working hand in hand, are going to solve the problems of poverty and oppression in this society.

This is a book for people who believe in people, in their dignity, in their determination, in their capabilities. It is for those who believe deeply that the problems of poor people will be solved by poor people working together.

Many of the terms in this book have been used so long that they have acquired more meanings than any term is entitled to. I have tried to let my definitions of "power structure," "community," "organizing," "communication," "organizer," "leader," and many others emerge in the course of the book. If there were other words to use, I would have preferred them. It will be helpful to realize that each of these terms will have different meanings in different situations. Each person will have to define these terms according to her own beliefs and experience, because this is how she will arrive at the definitions that will have meaning to her.

I have used the term "poor people" to mean any oppressed, dispossessed, or exploited group within this society. I could as easily have used poor white people, black people, Indians, Chicanos, students, draftees, miners, maids, women, welfare recipients, older people, or any of the other oppressed or exploited groups for whom organizing is meaningful. I hope each person will read this book in the light of his own experience and will mentally substitute for poor people his own group or the group he is working with, whatever it may be.

The ideas in this book are not mine alone. They belong to the poor people of the South and to the organizers who have worked with them. It is my great pleasure and privilege to have known them. I would like to think that by the time their children are old enough to read this book, it will no longer be necessary.

Mineral Bluff, Georgia   Si Kahn
1969

Preface to the Revised Edition

About to turn the corner of my 50th year, I am startled to see him suddenly standing directly in front of me: half my age, rail thin, blue work shirt rolled over his triceps, pouch of chewing tobacco in his hip pocket.

"So," he asks, "did you like the book?"

"Pretty much," I answer. "A lot more than I thought I would, given how much time has gone by."

"Thanks," he says. "Did you change it very much?"

"Not much at all. Mostly a few pronouns that would have embarrassed us both. The language has changed for the better in 25 years."

"And you?" he asks. "Have you changed?"

"Not my politics, if that's what you mean," I reply. "Except that I do trust poor and working people more—and people in power less."

"Glad to hear that," he says. "It's good to know you're still trying to hang in there."

He starts to turn away, then with a stubborn grin looks straight back at me: "Just don't ever forget where you came from."

Charlotte, North Carolina   Si Kahn
1994

Introduction

Survival Is Not an Academic Skill

By Chandra Talpade Mohanty

Those of us who stand outside the circle of this society's definition of acceptable women; those of us who have been forged in the crucibles of difference—those of us who are poor, who are lesbians, who are Black, who are older—know that *survival is not an academic skill*. It is learning how to stand alone, unpopular and sometimes reviled, and how to make common cause with those others identified as outside the structures in order to define and seek a world in which we can all flourish. It is learning how to take our differences and make them strengths. *For the master's tools will never dismantle the master's house.* They may allow us temporarily to beat him at his own game, but they will never enable us to bring about genuine change.

Audre Lorde, 1984*

Genuine change results from fighting power and domination, using and modifying the master's tools, creating our own tools. Genuine change must be demanded and worked for; it is never a gift. Audre

---

*Lorde, A. (1984). The master's tools will never dismantle the master's house. In A. Lorde, *Sister outsider* (pp. 110–113, esp. p. 112). Freedom, CA: Crossing Press.

Lorde died in 1992, but her wisdom and inspiration are a constant presence in my life. I begin with her words because they suggest the urgency of fighting back, of learning to be a warrior in the struggle against the exploitation and injustice that are so endemic to late-20th-century North America.

Si Kahn is one such warrior. He shows us how to fight, how to demand change, how to survive and make our dreams come true—how, in a word, to organize. *How People Get Power* is a modest book with an entirely immodest and appropriately ambitious vision. It shows us how to go about changing the world in the interests of its most disenfranchised citizens.

A couple of years ago, Si Kahn, Grassroots Leadership—the organization he founded in 1980—and the word "organizing" entered my social and intellectual world and lexicon. As an educator involved in thinking and teaching about social justice, and as a feminist of color in the American academy, I have always believed in activism as a necessary form of resistance to the business-as-usual attitude of educational institutions. However, Si's work—his music, organizing, and writing—has pushed me to think in new ways. It has enabled me to think about what the commitment to understand the systemic and psychic workings of power and domination and the courage and ability to act to empower poor and disenfranchised people might mean for educators. I'd like to suggest some ways that educators can benefit, learn from, and be challenged by this book. I believe that organizing, defined in the sharply astute, simultaneously utopian and realistic way in which Si Kahn speaks of it, is central to our rethinking of the meanings of activism in higher education.

I believe schools are not just instructional sites, they are also profoundly about the creation of ideas about the self, identity, community, and nation. Educational institutions produce and reproduce relations of knowledge and power, notions of justice and democracy. And except for a few experimental socialist schools in the early part of this century, and the freedom school movement that is part of the oppositional history of American education, most schools in 1994 are not places that work to empower women, poor people, people of color, and gays and lesbians. *How People Get Power* contains many enduring lessons for educators as well as community organizers. A book that encapsulates a different historical moment (late 1960s to early 1970s) from the one we are in in 1994 still endures because of its remarkable clarity of analysis and because, as Si says, fighting for freedom is a way of life, not a narrowly defined political goal:

> Freedom is a "habit of resistance"
> an acquired taste for saying "no" to injustice
> a conditioned reflex
> for helping others
> stand up and speak out
>
> Freedom is not
> the safe harbor
> at the end of the journey
>
> Freedom is the journey itself
> every day of our lives
> every step of the way

"Organizing," the way Si Kahn talks about it, draws attention to two crucial elements of activism: (1) the fact that we work collectively to resist domination, but that this working together is based on careful and detailed analysis of the social, cultural, and political context we find ourselves in and (2) the significance of beginning the work of organizing at the precise psychic, experiential, and ideological place people are in—not the place we want them to be in.

Perhaps what is singularly helpful for educators is this pedagogic insistence on the importance of research and analysis prior to the actual work of organizing (see especially chapters 1 and 2, Entering the Community and Sizing Up the Community) and the emphasis on *building* rather than merely *assuming* a shared consciousness of the best way to organize to combat injustice. An organizer is always a teacher, but she is a teacher who works with her constituency in such a way that she is no longer necessary to the struggle:

The organizer must always remember that eventually she must leave the community and that whatever roles she fills will be vacated when she leaves. Her responsibility is not to be a leader of the poor, but to work with the poor community while it develops leaders of its own; not to be a spokesperson for the poor, but to help them speak for themselves. (p. 49)

This is one of the hardest lessons for teachers, albeit one that many of us take for granted as integral to our practice. To teach in a way that undermines dependencies, especially on the part of marginalized learners, and actually leads to autonomy and self-directed thinking and action in struggles for social justice is very hard indeed. It requires foresight, a commitment to a radical shift in power relations in educational settings, and above all, the understanding that as teachers often working against the mandate of the institutions that employ us, we will be penalized (not rewarded!) for such activist teaching. These acts of dissent are profoundly contrary to the professionalism (or conformity) expected of educators. Of course, there is a great deal of difference in organizing a poor people's organization and organizing to create and sustain a culture of dissent and possibility in educational institutions. Schools are places that bring girls and boys, women and men, of different socio-economic backgrounds, cultures, and races together to work on a common curriculum. In this situation, it won't work to create organizations based on the demands and needs of one particular constituency. However, as educators we can draw upon and develop an insight Si Kahn offers his readers. We can begin our exploration and understanding of the way power operates in the world from the day-to-day experience of its most disenfranchised people, rather than from the point of view of the elite. We can ask our questions with the interests of marginalized people at the center of our field of vision. In this way, thinking, learning about, and working toward building poor people's organizations can provide an essential point of entry for educators working to understand and dismantle oppressive power relations.

In learning the lessons of this text—that (1) place, space, history, and culture are fundamental to building successful organizations to fight injustice; that (2) creating a sense of solidarity and community, and a culture of resistance, is central to consolidating and maintaining collective struggles; and that (3) developing indigenous leadership is absolutely essential if we are to sustain any long-term struggle for power—we will have learned a great deal about what it takes to bring about fundamental social change. This is the gift Si Kahn offers educators in this book. This is not just a book about organizing oppressed communities in the 1960s; it is about what it takes to understand and analyze the political and cultural operation of power during the civil rights movement, and the continuities and discontinuities between our understanding of power then and now, between the tactics of the 1950s and 1960s and what is required to bring about sustained economic and political change for the poor and the oppressed in the 1990s.

At a time (post Reagan/Bush) when democratic citizenship appears to have been emptied of its participatory, egalitarian, and visionary meanings, and activism is most immediately recognizable in the strategies of the Right to Life movement rather than in the work of the labor, racial, ethnic, or women's movements, a book that takes us to the root of the problem and teaches us that collective grassroots organizing must be at the center of meaningful social change is both rare and invaluable. For above all, Si Kahn expresses a profound belief in the capacity we all have for self-determination even in the most oppressive of conditions, the capacity to imagine, and to struggle for, our collective freedom and autonomy:

> I believe that a person's capacity for leadership
> is often in inverse proportion
> to the discrimination and exclusion
> they have personally experienced—
> which explains why, in our time
> so much visionary and transforming leadership
> has come from African Americans

and other people of color
from women of different colors and classes
from poor and working people of different races

I believe that in the end
those who are now excluded and exploited
will get what they deserve
only through their own action
by organizing together
by building collective power
and by demanding change

Perhaps this is why I am so moved by *How People Get Power*. I, a woman of South Asian (Indian) origin, a feminist and antiracist educator in the United States who traces her origin to a postcolonial Third World country, and Si Kahn, a white Jewish American organizer and musician who traces his origin and history to struggles against racism and antisemitism in the United States, not only sit together, we learn from each other, fight side by side, and envision a new world based on a radically different set of values from those of the dominant culture. This is possible because of the power of the ideas, analyses, strategies, and vision Si Kahn defines in this book. Even with the obvious differences in our histories and experiences, Si and I share the strength and inspiration of a vision, a dream of genuine change. In this book Si teaches us how to work toward this dream. I urge educators concerned about social justice to read this book, to use it in their lives, and to share its message and its vision generously with others.

 Chapter 1

Entering the Community

For many years now, people in this society have been hearing about the conditions of poverty and oppression that exist within it. Some have listened more closely than others and, moved by what they have heard, have begun working with poor and oppressed people to help them change the conditions of their lives. Almost all these people have been sincere, dedicated, and well-meaning. Few of them have possessed the knowledge, experience, and skills to work effectively as organizers.

Organizing is a technique, not a mystique. For all the romance about organizing, it is a discipline like any other. Some of the things that go into making an organizer are born with her; most can be learned. There are skills, techniques, and methods that have been developed by past organizers that have shown their effectiveness in numerous communities. The person who goes into a community without having taken the time to learn them may mean well, but she will have a hard time doing as well as she might have. Like any other professional, the organizer must understand and follow certain procedures if she is to be effective.

The first decision an organizer has to make is how and when to enter a community. In some ways, this will be the most basic decision the organizer makes in her work, because everything she does after she arrives in a community will be influenced by the initial impression she makes and by how the community reacts to her.

During the entry period, the organizer must make such basic decisions as who her first contacts in the community will be; which parts of the community she will try to communicate with and which, if any, she will try to avoid; where she will live; how she will dress; how she will talk; and how she will explain to people in the community what she is trying to do. She may later change her mind about the way she wants to do some of these things, but for the most part, as far as people in the community are concerned, she will continue to be seen in terms of the initial impression she makes. An organizer has the chance to enter a particular community for the first time only once, and the mistakes she makes will stay with her as long as she is there.

It is easy to underestimate the effect that the arrival of an organizer can have on a community. Communities, and especially small rural ones, tend to have fairly stable social structures. Of course, relationships among people in the community will change, but generally the people in the community are known to each other. The organizer represents an element that is new in the community, that is unknown. She is above all a stranger. Out of curiosity, out of defensiveness, out of political and social habit, the community will react to the organizer's presence and will begin to analyze the organizer, her relationship to the community, and even the community's own relationships within itself.

For example, take a situation that was fairly common in the early days of the civil rights movement: A young, white, middle-class student from a northern college arrived in a small rural southern town and moved in with an African American family. The arrival of the organizer produced several immediate results, of which the most visible was hostility and even violence on the part of the white community. Sometimes this was directed against the organizer; more often against vulnerable members of the black community. As a result of this hostility, the organizer was cut off from the white community. Such possibilities as working directly with the power structure or organizing among the poor whites in the community were abruptly ruled out.

On the other hand, the arrival of the organizer often had immediate positive effects on the black community. By moving in with the people, the organizer identified himself with them—their problems, their hopes, their fears. Sometimes his arrival had an immediate catalytic effect on the community; now that they had an organizer among them, people felt, they could begin to take action. In other cases, the fact that in the beginning the organizer had identified with the people later caused the people to identify with him. Many direct-action campaigns began as a reaction to the beating or jailing of a popular organizer.

Most of these young organizers had not consciously developed a strategy for entering the community. In retrospect, however, it is possible to analyze the reasons why this approach was probably the best under the existing circumstances. In the Deep South in the early 1960s, few white people were willing to trust or even tolerate anyone working in the black community. Similarly, few black people could afford to trust anyone working with poor whites or with the white power structure. Even if the organizer had begun by working with the white power structure, whatever influence he gained with them would have been lost as soon as he began working in the black community. On the other hand, the hostility of the power structure to the organizer could often be helpful to him in gaining the acceptance of the black community. Under these conditions, little could be gained and much lost by attempting to work with the white community. Though not a planned strategy, the approach used was one that was usually successful in gaining the confidence of the poor community.

The proper time to make such an analysis, of course, is before the organizer enters the community he will be working in. "Community" here means those people the organizer is working with directly or intends to work with eventually. In the above example, the organizer defined his community as the poor black people in a particular area. Obviously this group is a subgroup of other communities: town, county, state, black people, poor people, and so forth, depending on the kind of definition one is interested in making. But as far as the organizer is concerned, the option of defining what a community is belongs to him. He can make it as large or as small as he feels is useful in terms of what he is trying to accomplish. Once he has defined this community, however, he must be prepared to work and deal with all of its members.

This is not to say that the problems of different groups in an area are not related. The problems of poor African Americans in a small southern town are closely related to those of the poor whites in that town; to the operation of the white power structure; and to political decision making on the town, county, state, and national levels. A good organizer will deal as well as she can with these different relationships. For example, it would probably be effective in the above situation to organize the poor whites in the area around some of the issues that they have in common with the poor blacks: un-employment, working conditions, housing, political representation, education. It would be necessary, however, to do this separately, using a different organizer from the one in the black community. Like it or not, good organizing today is being done almost entirely by organizers from the same background as the people they are working with: black people with black people, mountain people with mountain people, Chicanas with Chicanas, students with stu-dents, welfare mothers with welfare mothers. In situations where race is a factor, it helps to have one organizer of each race working in the different communities and maintaining contact with each other to develop strategies and tactics.

Unfortunately, few organizers will be allowed the chance to de-velop their strategy for entering a community before they actually begin working in it. Only a few organizers today have the freedom to choose in advance the community they want to work in, to ana-lyze it before entering it, and to put into practice all the strategies and techniques they have decided to use. Many organizers today work for agencies of one sort or another and are restricted by the rules, goals, and images of those groups. In most such cases, the organizer's main problem is how to distance herself from the poor image the agency has in the community. Most agencies supposedly set up to help poor people—welfare departments, employment agencies, community action agencies, and the like—have extremely poor reputations among poor people. In any case, the basic rule for entering a community still applies: The organizer must define her own role, even if it conflicts with that of her sponsoring agency, and develop her own strategies for putting it into action.

These strategies will depend as much as anything on the personality of the organizer. Generally, an effective organizer will have a good deal in common with the people she is working among. In the mountains of North Carolina, for example, it helps to know a lot about fishing, hunting, pulpwooding, farming, trucks, country music, quilting, canning, tobacco, shotguns, children, dogs, and religion. The reason is simple. Most of an organizer's time is spent talking with people, and people talk about the things they know. If an organizer does not share knowledge and experiences with the people she is working among, she will have a hard time communicating with them. Put bluntly, most good organizers have been extremely popular in the communities where they have worked. Again, the reasoning is simple: If people don't like you, they won't let you stay around long enough to organize them.

Given the choice, then, an organizer should choose a community to work in where she has as much in common with the people as possible. Usually, however, she won't have this choice. This is especially true of those who come to organizing from middle-class backgrounds. Some middle-class organizers have enough background in common with poor people to work and communicate with them immediately. If an organizer can "pass for poor," she can realistically plan to take a job in a factory and organize from within. But if, as is most always the case, her middle-class background shows through to the extent that the other factory workers would be immediately suspicious of her motives for working there, she would probably be better off working under some type of established sponsorship until she builds up her understanding of the poor community and the people in it.

The approach to be used in entering a community, then, will depend on both the community and the organizer, and on the organizer's analysis of the type of relationship that is realistically possible between her and the people in the community. The type of initial contact made should depend on this analysis, as well as on the purposes for which the organizer is entering the community. Regardless, it is absolutely necessary that the organizer gain the confidence of the poor people; otherwise there will be no way she can work with them effectively.

There are also reasons for making contact and establishing communications with the power structure. In some cases, it may be realistic to expect the power structure to eventually provide some of the things poor people want and need and to participate in the overall development of the community. This is especially true in small rural towns or counties that have little industry or agriculture. In areas like this, the "power structure" is often materially little better off than the poor people in the community generally (for example, in one Georgia county in 1960, there was no one with an annual income over $10,000). The mayor may also be a mechanic, and the city council may include a millworker, a retired rural mail carrier, an active mail carrier, and a warehouse worker. Although they do constitute the power structure, or at least the decision-making authority of the town, there is no real gap between them and the rest of the people. It would be shortsighted for an organizer to write these people off as power structure and ignore them, or worse, to deliberately alienate them. In this case, it is in their interest for the community as a whole to progress.

This is not true, however, in most communities where an organizer will be working, particularly when there are significant differences of race or class within the community. In areas where there are large numbers of poor people, maids, millworkers, tenant farmers, sharecroppers, miners, slum tenants, or credit buyers—meaning almost anywhere—the power structure will tend to oppose any effort to change the status quo. In such a situation, efforts to enlist the power structure's assistance will result in frustration, or worse, in changes that will hurt the poor people the organizer is working with.

Even in this situation, though, there are good reasons for maintaining as much contact as possible with the power structure. If there is a conflict between the interests of the poor people and those of the power structure—as there usually is—it is important for the organizer to know as much as possible about the people who are opposing him and what he is trying to do. By maintaining contact with the power structure, the organizer will have a chance to size up each of its members personally; to estimate their strengths and weaknesses; and as a result to develop an effective strategy with the poor people. "Know your enemy" is a good rule for organizers. In a conflict situation, the last people an organizer has to worry about are his friends.

Consider a situation, for example, where the organizer has been successful in gaining the trust of the mayor of a medium-sized town. A poor people's organization with which the organizer has been working calls for a demonstration. If the mayor contacts the organizer and asks for his estimate of the situation, the organizer can say, "I think it's serious, and it will probably get worse if the city doesn't do something about their demands." Sometimes a prod like this will convince a city or county government that it should take a demonstration seriously, when otherwise it might be inclined to ignore it.

A final reason for maintaining contact with the power structure applies in situations in which the power structure is openly hostile to the aims of poor people in the community. Often an organizer who is sophisticated in his dealings with the power structure can do much to neutralize this hostility. Sometimes, of course, hostility to the organizer and the people he is working with can help accelerate the process of organizing. People often respond when they feel they're being pushed too hard. But this should not be allowed to happen until the organizer has a firm base of support in the poor community. One of the first rules of organizing is, "Don't get run out of town." An organizer who regularly drops in to visit with members of the power structure, who is friendly, who occasionally helps them out in small ways, may still be hated for what he stands for, but he is less likely to be hated personally. If he can convince the power structure to at least tolerate him, he may be able to ward off some of the aggression that might otherwise fall on the poor people he is working with.

In most areas, the organizer will be accepted most easily by the poor people if he is living in the area where they live, provided that he seems to them the sort of person who would naturally be living in that area. An organizer living "on the right side of town" may be more readily accepted by the power structure, but at the same time this will hurt his acceptance by the poor community. Some organizers have successfully commuted into poor areas or lived in the area between the "right" and "wrong" sides of town. This is possible in many rural areas, where brick homes alternate with one-room shacks. (Often, of course, the owners of the shacks are the folks living in the brick homes.) But generally an organizer who is working with the people should live among the people.

How an organizer talks, and the way he presents himself generally, will have much to do with how he is accepted by different groups within the area. Honesty is the key. Yale undergraduates don't talk and act like Tennessee highlanders, and the organizer who tries to hide or disguise his background is asking for trouble. Of course, some organizers with college backgrounds are from rural areas and are comfortable talking "country." There is no reason for them not to do so, as long as they don't slip into Madison Avenue English from time to time. Whatever style of speech an organizer uses, it should be one he can maintain comfortably and in all situations. If an organizer has been talking country with the poor people and Harvardese with the power structure, he could be in an awkward situation if he had to talk with both groups at the same time. Whatever image the organizer presents should be one he is comfortable with and can comfortably maintain as long as he is in the community.

Making initial contacts can be a problem if the organizer comes into the area through the sponsorship of an agency, because he will probably not be able to choose which contacts he wants to make. Usually one of the heads of the agency will take him around and introduce him to "people in the community." Sometimes the agency will introduce him to militant poor people; more often, it will give him a guided tour of the power structure. All that an organizer can do in the latter situation is to grin and bear it and wait until he has made a good analysis of the community on his own before following up on any of these contacts.

The ideal situation is one in which the organizer has considerable time to study the community before moving into it. Occasionally an organizer will be working in one community and will choose a second one he plans to begin working in several months or a year later. He then has a chance to casually survey the area—driving through occasionally, stopping for meals, dropping into stores to buy a dollar's worth of anything, asking directions, shooting an occasional game of pool, stopping by beauty parlors and barber shops, drinking a beer, asking questions. In this way he can increase his knowledge of the community before he begins organizing there and also pave the way for his actual entry by becoming more or less a familiar face around town. By working slowly and carefully, he can develop a body of support for himself and his work before even coming into town.

The organizer's way of entering the community, then, should make it as easy as possible for the poor people in the community to accept and trust him. As much as he can, the organizer should try to be himself. But he should also realize that his standards may not be the standards of the community and that by indulging what he considers to be his personal freedoms, he is limiting the opportunities of the people he is supposed to be working with. If a person is not dedicated enough to be willing to limit some of his privileges in order to help other people achieve their rights, he has no business in organizing.

 Chapter 2

Sizing Up the Community

It is the organizer's responsibility, even before she enters a community, to analyze it as well as she can. This analysis helps her put the work she will be trying to do there into perspective and to understand some of the problems she will have to confront. Without a good analysis of the area, there is danger that, at best, the work the organizer does will be fragmentary and irrelevant to the actual problems of people in the community. At worst, the organizer's work may actually reinforce the conditions that make and keep people poor and powerless.

No one analysis can be made that will apply to all of the communities in which people are poor. In the mining counties of eastern Kentucky, the causes of poverty are close and contemporary: a local economy that depends on exploitation of the majority—the miners and their families—by a small minority—the coal operators. On the Native American reservations of the Southwest, the causes of poverty are historical: a national policy of systematic oppression and deprivation carried out almost to completion in the 18th and 19th centuries. Ultimately, the roots of poverty in the United States lie in a system of economic development that has denied rights and opportunities to those who could be denied them. There is sometimes a strategic distinction, however, between working with those who were victimized in previous periods of time and with those who are just now being exploited.

This distinction is important, because the degree to which the causes of poverty in an area are close and contemporary—that is, local—will determine the effectiveness of tactics that are developed and carried out on a local level. In a county where there is one major employer, employing hundreds of people at minimum wage, it is reasonable to think in terms of strategies designed to produce higher wages, comprehensive fringe benefits, and improved working conditions. In counties where there is no major employer, solutions to the problems of poverty must generally be looked for outside the area—bringing industry in, carrying people out to where jobs can be located, or causing higher levels of authority, federal or state, to assume responsibility for those who, on a national basis, have been left in the economic backwater. In terms of tactics, the distinction is between confrontation at the local level and self-help; between forcing those elements in the community that are capable of eliminating poverty to do their job, and where these elements do not exist and where the leverage to influence change at a higher level is lacking, developing local alternatives.

The preliminary analysis that an organizer makes of her community, then, is basically concerned with one question: Under ideal conditions, what could the community realistically provide in terms of decent living conditions for all its members? A number of more detailed questions may serve as guides in making this analysis. The following seven areas raise questions about current employment, other income, and political control:

1. How many people in the community are employed? For what wages?
2. How many people are unemployed? Are these people employable at jobs now existing within the community? Are they employable at jobs existing elsewhere?
3. Could wage levels in local industry reasonably be increased? For example, many nonunion metals plants in the South pay wages considerably below those of union plants in the same industry elsewhere in the country. On the other hand, the wage difference between union and nonunion textile mills in many areas is fairly small.

4. Is the community reasonably capable of attracting new industry? Is an effort to attract industry being made? If not, is a deliberate effort being made to exclude new industry to maintain a surplus labor pool and keep wages low?

5. What sources of income do the unemployed have? To what extent are these sources of income beyond the control of local politicians? To what extent are they within this control? To what extent is this being used as an element of political leverage?

6. What are the establishment's reasons for seeking political control of the community? How is this control exercised?

7. What percentage of the people are poor? What percentage are members of an ethnic group?

The answers to these questions will vary greatly depending on the community. For example, the seven answers for a county in Georgia's "Black Belt" might read—

1. Some 700 people are employed. About 150 are employed in two woodworking plants. About 150 are employed in pulpwood operations. About 200 work in agriculture at seasonal wages. About 100 are employed as maids. About 100 work out of the county. Wages range from slightly above the minimum wage for factory workers to significantly below for maids and agricultural workers.

2. Some 400 people are unemployed year-round. Of these, about 300 are women. About half the total are over age 40 and would not be hired by local industry. They could, however, be trained for work in other types of industry, such as textiles, that are not located in the area. Those under 40 could work in the local woodworking plants. However, these plants are working at capacity, and they hire only white male employees.

3. Local wages are considerably below national averages. The annual profits shown by the industries indicate that wages could be raised without impairing the ability of the industries to compete.

4. The community has all the assets that generally attract industry: highway, rail, and water transport; adequate electrical, water, and sewer facilities; industrial sites; a surplus labor pool. However, no attempts are being made to attract new industry.

Because 450 of the 600 persons employed in the county work at below minimum wage, it is reasonable to conclude that a deliberate attempt is being made to exclude new industry to maintain the surplus labor pool so that people will have to work at low wages as maids, agricultural workers, and pulpwood cutters.

5. Unemployed people exist mainly on social security and welfare. Because most jobs in the county are not covered by social security, the majority live on welfare. Members of the welfare board interlock with the county commissioners and their families and with the controlling interests in local industries. Local residents have attested that welfare and surplus commodities have been distributed on a "reward and punishment" basis: They are put on for voting "right," "docility," and "good behavior" and cut off for voting "wrong," "agitation," or general "troublemaking."

6. Profits from the locally owned industries depend on maintaining a group that can be exploited economically, by seasonal work, or by low wages. This in turn depends on keeping out new industry and on maintaining sufficient control over the labor pool to force its members to accept low-paying or seasonal work, by cutting off welfare and surplus food benefits. The use of these levers depends on political control of the county.

7. Sixty-five percent of the people are poor. Seventy percent are black.

From the analysis of this county, the organizer could draw several preliminary conclusions: that living conditions could be improved by forcing local employers to raise wages; that new industry could probably be attracted; that part of the key to this situation lies in political control of the county; and that political control could probably be achieved. The emphasis in any strategy that was developed would be on confrontation—forcing existing institutions in the community to live up to their capabilities—rather than on self-help.

For a second community, a mountain county in east-central Tennessee, answers to the seven question areas presented above might run as follows:

1. Little employment exists within the county. Those with transportation work in a large town about 40 miles east at wages

ranging from the minimum to very slightly above. About 50 people work within the county in gravel operations at minimum wage.

2. About half of the adults are unemployed. Most of these lack the skills to work in the heavy industrial plants outside the county. They could probably be trained for light industry, but these jobs do not exist in the area. There is almost no agricultural, timber, or domestic work.

3. Plants outside the county are unionized and pay wages at or above national average for the industry. The industries in the county—gravel pits—are marginal and probably could not absorb a wage increase.

4. Political and commercial leaders in the county have made a number of attempts to attract industry. However, the county lacks rail transport, there is no sewer system, the water system is inadequate, and the nearest airstrip is 40 miles away. No industrial sites have been developed. So far, no industries have shown any interest in moving in.

5. Unemployed people live on welfare and social security. Both are apparently reasonably administered. Very few instances have been reported in which these were used as elements of political pressure.

6. There is no real political establishment in the county. The major political figures are mostly small business owners. Few have been in office for any length of time. Many of the elected officials don't run for reelection. Most have made some attempts to develop the county.

7. Thirty-five percent of the county is poor. Four percent is African American.

In this situation, confrontation tactics at the local level would fail to produce significant results because the county does not contain the resources to provide a decent living for its residents. Confrontation tactics are basically aimed at the redistribution of wealth and other resources, and it is not always true that within a given community there is enough wealth to redistribute. The problem in this county is that it has been left out of the national economic mainstream. Although on the one hand it is true that this imbalance should be readjusted, on the other hand the county does not have within itself the potential leverage to force this change. In this situation, the strategy developed by the organizer would be aimed at self-help methods—at assisting the total community, including parts of the power structure, to develop itself.

There is a real need for the organizer to maintain freedom from preconceptions and dogmatized plans of action. One of the unique features of the political subdivisions within the United States is their diversity. There are states varying in population from 454,000 to nearly 30 million persons and cities, towns, and counties ranging from several hundred to several million. The power structures within these political subdivisions are equally diverse. It is important for the organizer to recognize that not all power structures are powerful, sophisticated, wealthy, or politically astute. In most counties, the county commissioners, sheriff, ordinary, clerk of courts, county judge, welfare director, school superintendent, health director, school principals, mayors, and city council members are generally considered in some way part of the power structure. If the county only has 5,000 persons in it to begin with and has to choose these 50-odd officials, the general level of ability is not likely to be too high. It is often also true that in such a county there is very little worth fighting over. This is not to say that there will not be fighting over what there is; political contests are just as hard fought in poor counties as in rich ones. But where there is little in the county to begin with, an organizer who can present realistic alternatives for developing the county as a whole can often persuade the members of the power structure that it is in their interest to cooperate with what he is trying to do. To put it another way, in a poor county the members of the power structure may also be, from a national point of view, among the exploited.

The differences among political subdivisions make very real the need for sophisticated community analysis. As far as possible, this should be done *before* the organizer enters the community. There are a large number of readily accessible sources that can be used, at a distance, to assist in the development of a good community analysis. Later, when the organizer has been working in the community for some time, he will want to make further analyses in greater depth and detail, on the basis of additional information that he can get only in the community or from personal contacts. However, he should still make the best possible analysis of the community at a distance, before he begins working in it.

One of the most basic sources of information is the U.S. Census. Census volumes are issued by state. Statistics can be obtained from these publications that are useful in developing a community analysis:

- County population; population of towns; breakdown of population by age and race.

- Income levels, broken down by categories. By doing some calculation, it is possible to come up with a figure for the total amount of money made (legally) in the county in a year. The distribution of categories is important: It helps to know that a county has no one earning over $20,000, or five people earning over $100,000.

- Employment, broken down by occupational groups. From this a good estimate can be made of the relative proportion of professional, skilled, semiskilled, and unskilled job slots in the county, as well as of the types of industry and other employers in the area.

From the census data, a number of important deductions can be made. In fact, a general economic profile of the county can be arrived at. The next step is to fill in the general outline with specific data. Much of this research can be done in the state capital. The state department of industrial development will usually have a list of all employers in the state, with generalized statistics such as number employed, major products, gross sales, and so forth. If this is not available, visit the local library and get a copy of one of the directories published by various national business associations. In some states, local area planning commissions publish detailed reviews of all local industries. If the plants are unionized, regional offices of the unions can often provide information.

The U.S. Department of Commerce, in cooperation with state highway departments, publishes detailed road maps for each county in the country. These are coded in great detail. In rural areas, they show sites of individual farms, houses, stores, schools, churches, post offices, state police barracks, prisons, filling stations, motels, factories, sawmills, radio stations, golf courses, gravel pits, and many other things. Considerable economic data not otherwise available can be obtained from these maps: miles of paved versus unpaved roads; number of houses on unpaved roads, often a key to the extent and distribution of poverty; number of vacant houses, often a key to migration patterns; concentration of paved roads in a particular section of the county, often a key to centers of political influence; concentrations of population, often a key to the independence or dependence of people in the community. These maps also list all incorporated and unincorporated communities in the county—something the organizer should memorize. By using these maps, the organizer can familiarize himself with the county before he even sees it.

As much time as possible should be spent in the files of the state newspaper that covers the particular area. The list of communities memorized from the county maps should be used as a guide—news stories will be preceded by the name of the community they come from. In particular, any names mentioned in news stories should be noted: Any person mentioned in a state release will in one way or another be prominent in her home county. Most state newspapers also carry a list of bills introduced by state representatives and senators while the legislature is in session. These can be a valuable clue to what the power structure of the county considers in its interest. Occasionally the libraries in the state capital will have on file back issues of newspapers from other areas. If the paper from the county the organizer is planning to enter is available, it can be an invaluable source of information. If not, the organizer should take the time after entering the community to research back issues of the paper with extreme care. In addition to news stories, legal notices, society pages, and even obituaries (an aid in uncovering kinship lines) can be valuable sources of information for the good researcher.

Most telephone companies will provide copies of local directories to people who can show a need for them. The listings in the yellow pages will provide the names of doctors, lawyers, dentists, optometrists, building contractors, department store owners, cotton gin operators, and others who are likely to be key figures within the power structure. As a very rough guide, the size of the ads for business and commercial enterprises can be taken as an indication of their relative importance. The listings by name in the front of the directory should be gone through carefully, and a count made of the individuals with each family name. This can be an important key to their relative importance and to kinship groups within the county. The telephone directory is an important social indicator: Those listed are not likely to be among the very poorest.

Whatever the situation under which an organizer goes into a community, the key to a successful entry is a careful analysis of the community, made beforehand. Through this analysis, the organizer can decide how he wants to go into the community and what he wants to do once he gets there.

 Chapter 3

Making Contacts

Once an organizer has actually begun working in a community on a regular basis, her next step is to gain its trust. This is necessary for two reasons. First, in most cases, the extent to which an organizer can influence the actions of a community will depend on how well she is trusted by its members. There are organizing tactics that are based on emotions rather than trust. In conflict situations, for example, organizers have deliberately intimidated groups into action, on the assumption that in the course of the action the group would develop its own motivations and impetus. This occurred many times in the early civil rights movement, when large numbers of people first developed a real understanding of what they were doing and why while being clubbed to the ground or pushed with a cattle prod. Situations like this have occurred mostly in "issue organizing," when an issue that could serve as a nucleus for people to come together around has appeared unexpectedly, and an organizer has moved in to take advantage of it. But such tactics would not ordinarily be used in a situation in which the organizer had already selected a community and made extensive preparations to move into it.

The second reason for gaining the trust of the community is to establish, as quickly as possible, a base of power. Once an organizer has gone into a community, her first responsibility is to stay there until she accomplishes what she set out to do, or, in some cases, until it has become certain that there is no way she can accomplish it. (Saying that the organizer sets out to accomplish certain goals does not mean that she decides in advance what the goals of the people in a community should be. An organizer's own goal should be to help people in the community achieve the things they see as important to their own lives.) In almost any situation where an organizer is working effectively, there will be pressure to get her out of the community. How effectively the organizer can counteract this pressure will depend on how well she has built up this base of power and support. This base may depend in part on her acceptance by elements of the power structure. More probably, the base will have its roots in the poor community.

One of the first rules of establishing trust between the organizer and the people is visibility. Communities tend to be most accepting of that which is most familiar. People individually behave the same way. If the people in a community feel that the organizer is well known to them, they will more readily accept her as part of the community. In a community where a good organizer has been working for some time, most people will overestimate by several years the length of time she has actually been there. This is a measure of how familiar the organizer has made herself to them. This familiarity is established by spending as much time as possible with people in the community, and in places where they spend their time.

The places where people congregate will differ from community to community. In most rural areas, the general store or country store functions as a natural community center. People come to the store not only to buy provisions but to get news, exchange gossip, play cards or checkers, and talk with friends. Most groups have a more or less set time they will appear at the store. The older men may come early in the morning to sit and warm up in front of the stove, female and male teenagers in the afternoon when school lets out to buy a Coke, the mill hands and pulpwooders in the early evening to play poker. Buying a soft drink or a candy bar is a ticket to spend as long as you want in the store, sitting on a bench or leaning against the wall, listening to the conversation. In good weather people will gather on the front porch. Time spent by the organizer sitting on the front porch of the general store is usually well spent; people walking or riding by will see him, and each time they see him they will become a little more used to his presence in the community. It is helpful for the organizer to have a regular time when he is at the store; people who want to get in touch with him will know when and where to find him.

Gas stations are also gathering places, particularly for teenagers and working people. Often the local general store doubles as the gas station if the community is small enough. In larger towns, where there are two or more stations, the organizer should spread his business among them. Most rural stations, if they have a grease rack, will let people use them to do a lube job or other work on their car or truck. Time spent under the rack working on his vehicle gives the organizer a chance to meet and talk with local people. Cafes, beer parlors, pool halls, barber shops, beauty parlors—any place people in the community gather is a good place for the organizer to spend time.

From time to time, communities will have special events that are worth attending. Auctions, dances, revivals, turkey shoots, drag races, football games, fish fries, chicken suppers, barbecues, trading days, gospel sings, country music festivals—all offer an opportunity to be seen and make new contacts, especially if the organizer is comfortable in these situations. By meeting people away from their homes, in places and situations that are basically neutral, the organizer has a chance to size up the people in the community and to find and develop a relationship with those people he needs as organizing contacts. Meetings of this type are extremely useful in broadening the range of acquaintances the organizer has within the community. To put it another way, he can talk with people in situations like these, where there are large numbers of people present, that he couldn't afford to be seen visiting privately.

Every community contains numerous, overlapping subgroups based on economic, political, social, and kinship relationships. If the organizer can gain the confidence of one or more key members of any group, his acceptance by its other members is fairly well assured. On the other hand, too close a connection with one group may result in rejection of the organizer by other groups that are in conflict with it. The organizer should become aware as soon as possible of the different factions within a community so that he can avoid too close an involvement in groups that might limit his acceptance by other elements of the community.

Once several key contacts have been developed, these can be used to develop other contacts within the community. Generally speaking, once the first few key contacts have been made, the organizer should not try to make other new contacts "cold." By this point, some of the people in the community with whom the organizer has been in closest contact should be developing a certain awareness of what he is trying to do. This is not always the case. Many very personable and likable individuals have gone into communities with the expressed intention of organizing them, have become very well accepted by the community, and have left without the community ever learning what they were there for—and without any organizing taking place. The organizer should begin early trying to develop with his contacts ideas for things that could happen in the community. These may be ideas that the people themselves contribute or that the organizer raises and people react favorably to. These ideas can then be used as tools to find other sympathetic contacts. The organizer can say things like "How about bringing me by to see some other folks who feel the same way we do?" or "Why don't you take me to see some folks you think can really be trusted about this?" In this way a network of key contacts sympathetic to the organizer's presence in the community, sharing certain concerns, and having a degree of mutual trust can be established.

Once the organizer has gained a reasonable footing in the community, he should rarely go places alone. Of course there will be times when the organizer will need to speak to people in private. But otherwise, the time an organizer has in a community is too valuable for him to spend it by himself. "Come with me" should be a stock phrase in his vocabulary. Whether the organizer is going to the county seat, to a nearby city, to the beauty parlor or barber shop, on a fishing or hunting trip, to the next town, or to a ball game, he should take someone from the community with him. People tend to talk more freely in a private atmosphere—in a car, in a kitchen, in a boat, in the woods. Trips like this give the organizer a chance to get to know the people he is working with better and give them a chance to get to know him. These trips also give him a chance to begin communicating to these people some of his ideas and to begin motivating them toward action.

Another reason for these close contacts is so people in the community can begin to understand the way the organizer operates and to move toward becoming organizers themselves. In many ways, the function of an organizer in a community is to produce other organizers. This is another way of saying that the organizer's role is to help bring forward new leaders within the community. The area in which an organizer is working is almost always too large for him to do all the footwork himself, and he will have to rely increasingly on the people working with him. In addition, the process of completely organizing a community—something that has probably never been done—takes an extremely long time, possibly 10 to 30 years. Few organizers will stay with one community for that length of time. When he does leave the community, the organizer must leave behind people who are committed to continuing the work of organizing and who also have the skills to do so. By working closely with his key contacts, the organizer is training them to eventually assume this role.

In some ways, the organizer's main job in the community in the early stages of organizing it is simply to make friends with the people there. That these friendships are also essential to the work of organizing the community does not mean that they are any less real. Most good organizers have a very real love and respect for the people they are working with and develop deep and lasting friendships with them. Many organizers, however, have a sense of uneasiness about these friendships because they feel they are in a way using these people to achieve their own goals. This need not be true as long as the organizer's main goal is to help people in the community achieve what *they* see as important to their lives. The organizer may not agree with what the community people want; her personal priorities may be very different from theirs. But she should always remember that however much she is accepted by people in the community, she never becomes a member of it. It is always their community, never hers, and she should never let her priorities override or undercut theirs.

In many situations, the organizer will also want to go about getting to know the power structure. This will be especially true when the organizer is employed by a group or agency that is in some way dependent on the power structure. Generally, because nearly every power structure, however monolithic it may appear, is highly factionalized, the organizer will be better off introducing herself to its members. One approach that is usually reasonably successful is to say something like "My name is Jane Smith, and I'm going to be working in the community trying to help people with their problems, and I thought" (or "I was told") "you could tell me what some of their problems are." Power structure people, like most other people, respond favorably when asked for advice, rather than when given it. Often the answer will be "We don't have any problems" or "We have a few problems, but we don't need any outsiders helping us solve them." Sometimes the answer will be something like "People are too sorry to work," "They're ignorant," "They're just plain lazy," or worse. No organizer will agree with these explanations, but there is little point in trying to argue about them. Power structures change their minds about poor people when confronted with group action and group pressure. If the organizer is working effectively, this will happen soon enough.

Each organizer will have to make her own list of those members of the power structure she feels are worth contacting. Such a list might include members of the governing authority of the county; mayors and city council members; city managers; the sheriff; county and municipal judges; school superintendents; welfare directors;

labor office managers; housing authority directors; urban renewal directors; public health directors and nurses; county agents and home economists; wardens; jailers; FBI officials; planning commission personnel; and members of the boards of education, welfare, and health agencies. In rural and agricultural areas, personnel of the U.S. Forest Service, fish and game commissions, the Soil Conservation Service (SCS), and the Agricultural Stabilization and Conservation Service (ASCS) may be important. Key private individuals might include lawyers, doctors, industry personnel managers, ministers, school principals, service organization heads, chamber of commerce personnel, and key members of electrical membership cooperatives (EMCs) and farmers' cooperatives.

Few organizers will see fit to contact even a majority of these persons. A complete list for even a small county would run to well over a hundred people, and the time involved in contacting all of them would be tremendous. There will also be a great difference in the relative importance of these people and in their relative value to the organizer. Few of them will be members of the power structure in the sense of having a major influence on decision making within the community. Most of them, however, can at one time or another be useful to the organizer. A surprising number of these individuals, particularly in areas where poor people constitute a potential political majority, are aware of the possibility of power shifts in the direction of control by the poor, and many are willing to cooperate in ways that might help their own political future. In addition, many of them will welcome any assistance that will help improve their image in the community or within their own federal or state department. Many agency heads in small communities are barely able to deal with the federal and state bureaucracies. The organizer who has a solid grounding in federal programs and who can help a local agency out—for example, by showing the people who run it how to get extra funds through a federal grant—can pick up useful support later on.

One important rule for organizers is that once a contact is made, it should almost never be broken. This is true in dealing with both the poor community and the power structure. A visit every few weeks to the government and agency people the organizer has made contact with can be helpful. If the organizer has accomplished things she knows will meet with power structure approval, she should let them know—it will often mean increased neutrality on the part of the power structure. Invitations to attend board meetings should be accepted, and poor people from the community should be brought along with the organizer when she goes. The organizer who can get inside county commission, city council, welfare board, board of health, and board of education meetings has a valuable chance to see key members of the power structure in action and to make her own judgments as to their strengths and weaknesses.

There is one major danger in dealing extensively with the power structure. Many organizers become after a time too much influenced by the power structure's interpretation of the problems of the community. Particularly in rural areas where the style of political leadership is rustic and rough cut, many organizers tend to underestimate the shrewdness and ability of members of the power structure. The first business of politics is still to get reelected, and many college-educated politicians with sophisticated ideas and abilities still look, talk, and act "country" in public. The fact that a county commissioner wears suspenders, chews tobacco, and spends most of his time talking about dogs and whiskey making does not mean that he is not an extremely tough and able politician or that there is anything deficient in his understanding of the people in his community. A good organizer never underestimates the people who oppose her or what she is doing.

Inevitably, an organizer whose goal is self-determination for poor people is in a sense "conning" the power structure when she attempts to gain its confidence. While she may believe that what she is trying to accomplish is in the long run best for the total community, she also has to recognize that it is usually contrary to what the power structure sees as in its own best interest. Just as inevitably, most power structures are very quick to see the threat to them that the organizer represents and will move to head her off. One of the ways of doing this is to con the organizer. In a situation like this, each party recognizes that the other is trying to use them and hopes that they are using the other party. When organizers and power structures have tried conning each other, the power structure has very often been the winner, usually because the organizer failed to believe that the power structure could use the same tactics she was using and use them as well or better. A good organizer always assumes that the other side is using all the tactics that she is and using them at least as well.

In many ways, the process of community organizing is a race against time. On the one hand, the organizer needs as much time as possible to build organized strength in the poor community. On the other hand, the power structure will move as quickly as possible to bring pressure on the organizer and on poor people in the community to prevent this from happening. It is important for the organizer to do everything she can to gain as much time as possible. The way in which she makes her initial contacts, in both the poor community and the power structure, has a great deal to do with whether or not she gets this time.

 Chapter 4

Bringing People Together

As the organizer works more and more with the people in the community, it should become increasingly apparent to her that their needs cannot be met by reliance on federally funded, locally controlled programs. These programs, which often have the result of increasing the dependence of those who are poor to begin with, are aimed at those who are already dependent: persons who are old, disabled, blind, or very young. For those poor people with the greatest chance to make a real change for the better in their lives— the teenagers, the young men and women—there is little or nothing.

It will also become apparent to the organizer that there is a limit to what can be accomplished by people working alone. An occasional poor person may win a welfare appeal or get put back on the food stamp program, but this does nothing to change the way the welfare system operates. In a mass society, in which power is exercised on a broad basis by methods of mass control, only group action is capable of applying the leverage necessary to change any of the ways in which the system functions. Years of single-handed efforts by courageous and determined individuals have proved only that such efforts can accomplish little against a power structure accustomed to absolute authority and willing to use any means necessary to maintain it.

The struggle between poor people and power structure is on a much more sophisticated level today than in the early days of the civil rights movement. At that time, the average power structure could be bluffed by militant speeches into yielding certain minimal concessions, or more usually, into overreacting to the point of physical violence, which had the almost inevitable effect of catalyzing, accelerating, and consolidating the struggle by poor people. Today only the most inexperienced power structure can be bluffed into such action. The strategy of most power structures today is to prevent such incidents from happening, out of a recognition that they are almost always turned to the advantage of the poor people's movement by the organizer. In recent demonstrations, police have even been used to restrain bystanders who might otherwise attack demonstrators and provide a further issue for the poor people's organization. If police power is used against the demonstrators, it is usually swift and massive. Occasionally the power structure is simply unable to restrain its own police force—a suggestion that the police may be becoming more of an independent force in this country than most people suspect.

The cold hard fact is that marches and picket lines don't scare anyone any more unless they represent and are a symbol for other types of power. Marches and picket lines are essentially social weapons; they are appeals to society, based on the assumption that society has a conscience and will act when injustice is pointed out. No organizer in this country would accept this point of view today. Social tactics are being abandoned in favor of economic, political, and violent measures. The struggle for the rights of poor people has moved into the power arena within American society.

The experiences of the civil rights movement are still a very strong influence on organizers today. Unfortunately, many of the tactics that had great success in the 1960s are no longer effective in most situations. It is hard today to recreate the highly charged emotional atmosphere in which the early civil rights workers operated. Action was produced by charismatic leadership, by techniques that might be better described as mobilizing than as organizing. Often, direct action began almost as soon as the organizer hit town. Communities had in many ways prepared themselves for the organizer; they knew what was happening in other places, wanted to be a part of it, and were just waiting for an organizer to show them what to do. In these situations, many organizers became leaders of and spokespersons for the communities they were working in. Because power structures moved quickly to try to contain and control the growing movement in the community, the organizer could depend on conflict situations developing in which community people would have the chance to gain experience quickly, to become hardened and motivated.

These types of tactics, used today, are still occasionally effective, especially in areas where they have not been used before. But generally they remain tactics designed for the achievement of limited social ends. The tactics of the early civil rights movement were designed to achieve the right to sit at a lunch counter, the right to sit in the front of the bus, the right to vote. They were not meant to help poor people achieve economic and political control of their communities. Today, it is understood that significant economic and political influence by poor people is an absolute necessity if their lives are to be changed for the better in any measurable degree. To achieve this kind of power, the organizer must work toward developing broadly based poor people's organizations. These must be organizations that involve as many poor people as possible, that involve them in deep and significant ways, in which leadership is widely shared, and in which the organizer plays as small a role as possible.

A good poor people's organization must be developed very slowly and with great care. If the organization expands too rapidly, many members will have little idea what the organization is about, nor will they have any real voice in deciding what the organization should be about. Because those with leadership potential need time to develop it and because leadership positions open up quickly, old-line "leaders" can step in and divert the organization from the purposes of the poor people. Membership will expand without direction, allowing many people to come into the organization who are against its real purposes and whose main reason for joining is to report to the power structure on what takes place. Because other people lack experience, the organizer will have too large a role within the organization and may end up manipulating it to a great extent. Organizations that are put together quickly also tend to lack the mutual trust and interdependence that give an organization internal strength. If the kingpin of the organization—such as the organizer himself—is pulled out, collapse will often soon follow.

To avoid these problems, the organizer must bring people together in such a way as to create mutual trust, interdependence, broadly based membership, and diversified leadership; to exclude from the organization those who might work against its goals; and to minimize his own role in it. The time in which he is actively working toward the creation of such an organization may well be his most difficult period within the community. His success will depend in large part on how well he has analyzed the community, how broad and how good his contacts are within it, how much pressure or freedom of action he has from the power structure, and how much trust he has been able to develop between key community people and himself.

A good starting point is often to make a list, mental or written, of the poor people the organizer considers to be potential leaders of the community. He can then begin to bring these people together, at first two at a time, later in groups, around the issues that have emerged in his earlier contacts with them. Many of these people will have known each other for years, and their own relationships will be different from the relationship any of them has with the organizer. As they begin to come together through the organizer, though, they will also begin to see each other partially in terms of their individual relationships to him.

This is a very important factor in the whole process of organizing. The presence of an individual identified as an organizer is often enough to force individuals, couples, groups, and communities to reexamine themselves and their relationships and to change these relationships. The fact that a person identified as an organizer has come to the community is in itself a statement that the structure of the community is not what it should or could be. Especially if the organizer is a charismatic individual, his very presence in the community will have a catalytic effect: It will force the community to begin changing in spite of itself.

As an example, suppose that the organizer has developed a close relationship with two women in the community who have themselves been friends for years. In their conversations with the organizer, both have expressed to her their concern with conditions in the housing project where they live. The organizer in turn has told the two about what has happened in other communities when public housing tenants got together and took action. One evening, while talking with one of the women, she says, "Look, I was talking to a woman down the street from you this morning about the same thing, and she sounded like she might be ready to move. Why don't we go by her place and see what she has to say?" Talking together with the organizer, the two women begin to experience their own relationship with an added dimension. Through the organizer as catalyst, they become potential partners and leaders in a group that has potential relevance to each of their lives.

The organizer will use variations of this technique to bring together those people she feels need to know each other in the sense of sharing the experiences and conversations they have shared with her. How she brings these people together will vary. She may be driving to town with one person and say, "Hey, I promised to bring someone else into town this evening. Mind if I go by and pick her up?" She may ask two people to come by the same place at the same time—a cafe, a restaurant, her home. Whatever the specific technique used, the basic process involves creating situations in which those people the organizer feels need to get to know each other can do so.

There are different ways the organizer can proceed from the basic technique of bringing people together. In situations that may develop a high degree of conflict and in which aggressive, confidential planning is necessary, the initial group may be developed by adding one person at a time. The organizer and one other person, usually the person she feels shows the greatest leadership potential within the community, will select a third person they both feel they can have complete confidence in. The three would then select a fourth, the four a fifth, and so on. Such a technique would be used in a situation when considerable power was at stake and when a high degree of mobility and secrecy was necessary.

One general technique that has proved highly manageable is block organizing. Although it is usually an urban technique, the same principles are often used in rural areas, although not under any particular name. In this technique, the community is divided by the organizer into areas that she feels have a certain natural cohesiveness and that are in effect subcommunities. These may actually be blocks in a town; more often, the divisions will cross artificial barriers like block lines. A typical block might consist of the families living in a "hollow" or tenement, the families living along a rural creek or road, the members of a "quarters" or barrio, or the tenants in a housing project. In each block, the organizer brings people together to form a block organization. These organizations in turn send representatives to a central poor people's organization. The block organization may take action on its own or in combination with other block organizations.

This method is very flexible and has a number of other advantages. It combines the interdependence and trust of a small group with the power and leverage of a large organization. Because block organization more or less follows classical lines of political organization, the transition to political action can easily be made. The block organizations are small enough to respond to local problems that may not seem important to members of the larger organization but that are important to people on the block. The relation between the poor people's organizations and its component block clubs makes for good communication.

Block organizing also fits in with the need for dispersal in organizing. The civil rights movement relied heavily on mass meetings as a way of welding people together, communicating information, and developing motivation and impetus. The disadvantages of the mass meeting are that there are limited opportunities for individual participation and that the power structure has a chance to measure the support the poor people's organization has. Real power in the world today is measured in numbers: number of votes, number of dollars, number of guns. A good organizer will not give her opponents the chance to estimate the degree of strength she is developing. It is much more difficult to estimate the number of persons attending 30 different block meetings, at irregular times and in different places, than to count noses at a mass meeting.

Small meetings also give the people in the community more of a chance to participate in the development of their own organization. In a large meeting, many people will be fearful of speaking out, because of shyness or out of fear of reprisals, when what they say is reported back to the power structure. In a small meeting, everyone present can be made to feel important and to feel that he or she can speak freely without fear of retaliation.

There will still be situations in which issues will arise unexpectedly and organizers will use mobilizing tactics to assist the community in dealing with them. But in long-term community organizing, the slow, deliberate building of a poor people's organization is one of the organizer's most important responsibilities. Like entering a community, building an organization is something the organizer can do only once. How well she does it will determine how effective it becomes.

 Chapter 5

Developing Leadership

It has been suggested earlier that one of the organizer's most important responsibilities within a community is to train local people as organizers, to give them the skills and knowledge he himself has, so that they will be able to take over his functions in the community when he leaves. Many of these people, being, unlike the organizer, members of the poor community, will also become its new leaders. Part of the organizer's job is to help these people develop the type of leadership qualities that will make them effective in broadening and consolidating the power of the poor within their community.

Traditionally, leadership in poor communities has been selected, trained, and maintained from the outside, that is, by the power structure. Sometimes "leaders" were handpicked from within the poor community itself, sometimes not. Whichever, because the power structure tended to feel that any effective leadership had to be patterned after its own image, these leaders tended to reflect in their personal lives and public conduct the values and characteristics of the power structure itself. They were expected to follow the power structure's lead in manner of speech, in style of dress, in use of tactics. To boost them economically, they were given jobs within the power structure as teachers, school principals, small business-people in the poor neighborhoods—jobs whose maintenance depended on the leaders' reliability in terms of loyalty to the power structure and ability to control the social, economic, and political actions of the poor. Such leaders were not representatives of the poor to the power structure, but representatives of the power structure within the poor community.

The power structure would channel through these leaders any rewards, however small, given to the poor community for approved social, economic, and political behavior—a few jobs, a road, an occasional new school or playground. If the poor ever attempted to go to the power structure directly, they were met with comments such as "You've got leaders—why don't you go to them?" At such periods, when the power structure's leaders seemed in danger of losing their hold over the poor community, they were reinforced by retaliatory measures against those poor people who were stepping out of line or by a new favor to the poor community to demonstrate its leaders' continued effectiveness.

By such deliberate reinforcement of its own concepts of leadership within the poor community, the power structure was also able to convince the poor community that, by and large, any new leadership group would have to conform to the pattern the power structure had established. Your leaders, the poor community was in effect told, must be people you can be "proud of": well dressed, well housed, educated, articulate. By implication, a poor person, a woman who wore cotton print dresses, a man who wore overalls and work shoes, who stumbled in speaking and used "ain't" instead of "isn't," who lived in a shack instead of a brick house, who walked instead of riding in a Chrysler, who worked in a field or mill instead of an office or classroom, had no business representing herself or himself in the centers of power. Any hint of the most basic ideas inherent in the concept of poor people's power, that each person is her or his own best representative and that the spokespeople for any group must come from within that group itself, was totally lacking.

As poor people's organizations began to develop, the power structure's leaders attempted to insinuate themselves into positions of leadership within the organization. In conflict situations, they appointed themselves to represent the poor community in negotiations with the power structure. If a situation developed in which direct-action tactics were used, these leaders were called together by the power structure to discuss what might be done to restore "peace and tranquility" or "law and order." Rarely in such negotiations were the real interests of the poor aggressively represented; even more rarely were the concessions granted by the power structure to the poor community, if any, more than the bare minimum that was considered necessary to stabilize the situation.

As poor people's organizations grew in strength and militancy, however, people began to reject such leadership. Poor people began to demand the right to speak for themselves, to represent themselves, to select their own representatives and negotiators. To establish the principle of self-representation, it became necessary to undercut the power of the power structure's leaders. Because this power was based on the leaders' ability to control the poor community, the tactic poor people used was to demonstrate that this control could no longer be effectively exercised. In one situation, for example, a boycott of downtown merchants was in effect. The leaders, without first consulting the pickets, met with members of the power structure and agreed to stop the boycott and withdraw picket lines from the stores in return for certain nominal concessions. When the stores opened for business the next day, the picket lines were still there. When those on the picket line were accused of violating the agreement, their answer was simply and truthfully, "Nobody's talked to *us*." In this situation, the poor people involved in the boycott not only established the principle of direct representation, that they alone had the right to speak and negotiate for themselves, they also successfully undercut the power of the "established leaders" by undermining the power structure's faith in these leaders' ability to control the poor community they supposedly represented.

In those communities where strong poor people's organizations have existed for some time, the principle of direct representation often has been established. More often, especially in counties that have not been organized before, the organizer will find that the leaders of the poor community are still those selected and approved by the power structure. One of the organizer's goals in such a situation will be to help the poor community undercut the power of the established leaders and to develop a new set of leaders from within the poor community itself.

As a first step, it will be necessary to identify these leaders, to help the poor community develop an understanding of the actual role they play, and to move toward undercutting their power. Often an easy way of identifying them is to ask key members of the power structure who the "responsible leaders and spokespeople" of the poor community are. Those who are identified as such by the power structure will usually be people who are influenced or controlled by the power structure and who represent its interests. On the other hand, those identified by the power structure as "troublemakers," "agitators," "outsiders," "irresponsible," "sorry," "out for them-selves," or "a discredit to their race" will often turn out to be real leaders of the poor, a part of and in touch with the poor community.

In her dealings with the "established leaders" as much as in her relations with members of the power structure, the organizer should be careful not to underestimate their ability to manipulate power and individuals shrewdly. Just as many members of the power structure talk and act "country" to get votes, many of the so-called leaders of the poor will speak with extreme militancy. Experienced manipulators of power are always careful to adopt whatever public mannerisms seem most likely to gain general sup-port at a given time. Many power structures have, in the past few years, developed a definite preference for militant rhetoric over mil-itant action. They have come to understand that "telling it like it is" may be one of the ways by which leaders of the poor who remain basically committed to the goals and values of the power structure maintain their control over the poor community. The power struc-tures are prepared to tolerate this rhetoric, even to their faces, rather than make concessions that might hurt them economically. The organizer must always, in judging individuals, go beyond the way they talk to the way they act.

One important characteristic of the established leaders of poor people is that they, like the power structure, have a high stake in what is often referred to as "the welfare of the community as a whole." This usually means, of course, the well-being of those who have it, whether a majority or a minority, at whatever cost to those who do not—in other words, the status quo. Unlike the poor, who, when they move, have only to "put out the fire and call the dog," the established leaders have homes, jobs, and business interests they cannot afford to lose. Many of them, holding their jobs as favors from the power structure, are well aware that their qualifications would not permit them to find such well-paying employment anywhere else if they were forced to move. Consequently they will oppose, openly or secretly, any change within the community that might threaten their privileged positions. In practice, this means that the established leaders will tend to oppose anything that might change the exploitative relationship between the power structure and the poor community.

It follows, then, that often many of the most effective leaders of poor people will be among those who have the least stake in the community, who have little or nothing to lose. The possession of material goods tends to make people conservative; the fear of losing what they have prevents them from acting in situations in which risk is involved. Those who have little or nothing are often free from these fears. In conflict situations during the past 10 years, an unusually high proportion of those who have emerged as effective and outspoken leaders of the poor community have been those who would generally be considered socially unacceptable by the power structure and its allies: persons who are unemployed or disabled, dropouts, pool sharks, hustlers, or ex-offenders.

A second group within the poor community from which effective leadership has often emerged consists of those who have income that is independent of pressure from the power structure. Such people might include owners of small businesses whose customers are mostly members of the poor community and those who draw checks from federal sources, such as social security and Veterans

Administration recipients. In rural areas, small farmers who own their land often are very independent and have good leadership potential. The more independent poor people in rural counties often live in the most rural areas, where they are not subject to the daily contact with the power structure that forces poor people in the towns to develop the dependent traits necessary for self-preservation.

Most organizers, in choosing those whom they regard as having leadership potential, tend to project their own personalities onto the situations they are dealing with. Many organizers, for example, find it difficult to communicate with people outside their own age group. As a result, the leaders who emerge in the communities these organizers are working in are often the same general age as the organizer. The organizer must make a conscious effort to avoid this type of preselection. For example, many leaders of the civil rights movement were teenagers. In rural areas, the vast majority of young people leave the community as soon as they have finished high school, if they finish. Anticipating this, they do not feel the same stake in the continued "stability" of the community that their parents and others of that age group have. This is not to say that there will not be many older people who will emerge as leaders. Many of those whose children have grown up and left town also develop a sense of having little to lose and as a result are willing to take risks that those with homes and families are not willing to expose themselves to.

While it is inevitable that the organizer will make some selections of those whose leadership potential she will try to develop, it is advisable to narrow the choice as little as possible. A poor people's organization needs a broad leadership group rather than a few persons in whose hands power is concentrated. The larger the group, the more time there will be for those who need the chance to develop their own particular leadership skills and to gain confidence in their ability to use them.

The process of developing leadership is mostly one of involving others in the process of planning and decision making. The organizer should take pains to involve potential leaders in this process whenever possible. Whenever she is making contacts, visiting agencies, or attending meetings, one or more of these people should go with her. As they begin to develop an understanding of what the organizer is doing, they should be given the chance to try out these skills themselves: to make rounds in the community, to go with other poor people to visit agencies, to conduct meetings, to plan strategy, to negotiate. As they gain in skill and confidence, their dependence on the organizer must decrease.

In the process of learning, experience is far more valuable than explanation. Many poor people, never having seen situations in which poor people have acted for themselves and won major victories, will doubt the possibility of this happening in their own community. The organizer should create opportunities for poor people to visit other areas where these things have taken place, so that they can talk with other poor people who have successfully faced problems similar to their own. The experience of meeting with members of poor people's organizations that have already been through what a new organization faces will do much to increase confidence and to combat the sense of isolation that poor people in difficult situations often feel. In addition, the links that are developed among different poor communities can eventually serve as a framework to interlock these communities in their common struggle for their rights as citizens and as human beings.

 Chapter 6

Working with Organizations

The process of working with a poor people's organization is very different from that of working with organizations of other types. The values that characterize other organizations common within the U.S. social, political, and economic structure frequently do not apply to poor people's organizations. Many persons with so-called "organizational backgrounds" who have attempted to work with poor people's organizations and who have tried to make them conform to traditional organizational patterns have often seriously harmed or even destroyed these organizations.

For example, one of the characteristic values of corporate organizations is efficiency. *Efficiency* usually means speed and accuracy in decision making and production. Key executives are expected to respond swiftly and decisively to critical situations. They are expected to represent and speak for their organizations. They also have the assurance that as long as they successfully represent the interests of the organization, those in power will support their actions. Generally, the membership of such an organization has no real desire to participate in the decision-making process at the power level. If it does have such a desire, it will be strongly discouraged. This type of organizational structure is in essence authoritarian; it stresses such key corporate values as authority, hierarchy, and centralized power.

In a poor people's organization, in which the goal is not profit for the few but power for the many, the above structure and values would produce results counter to the purposes of the organization. Power *for* the poor as a group is achieved through the exercise of power *by* the poor as a group. This is not a circular statement, but a realistic description of the way a poor people's organization tries to operate: by using power of one type—the power of the vote, the power to buy selectively or boycott, the power to disrupt the normal functioning of society—to achieve power of other types—power over the distribution of wealth, power over the means of production and distribution. The potential power of a poor people's organization is measured in numbers; it is broadly based rather than concentrated, decentralized rather than centralized. The power tactics a poor people's organization can use—strikes, boycotts, elections—depend on the broad support and participation of a large number of people. If the members of the organization are not given the opportunity to participate in the decision-making process, they will be less likely to understand and involve themselves in the exercise of power.

This means that the key value in decision making within a poor people's organization is not efficiency, but participation. The time required to reach a decision should not be the shortest time required for a small, select group to make the decision, but the amount of time it takes to educate all members in the meaning of the decision and to involve them with understanding in the decision-making process. Poor people, having been cut off from the centers of power within this society, are unaccustomed to the exercise of power or the use of power tactics. The organizer must make this type of membership education one of his main priorities in working with a poor people's organization.

The process of membership education involves slow and patient work with groups small enough for people to interact and interrelate. If the poor people's organization was originally organized along block lines, the block clubs can serve as the focus for this activity. If the organization began as a single small group and has expanded so that discussion in depth is no longer possible with all members present, it may be necessary to break the organization back down, for these purposes at least, into smaller groups. If the organization is countywide, for example, the members from each town or township could meet together. Often, when an organization becomes this large, it is useful for each of these subgroups to elect two or three persons, perhaps on a rotating basis, to serve on a steering committee. In a typical decision-making operation, the organizer would first meet with the steering committee to analyze the problem, form possible strategies, evaluate potential results, and put together alternative courses of action. The representatives from each of the subgroups, once they understood what was involved in the decision to be made, would meet with their own groups, with or without the organizer, and discuss the same points that had been gone over in the steering committee. When all these meetings had been held and it appeared to the organizer and the steering committee members that the other members had a good understanding of the situation, the organizer and the steering committee would meet again to rediscuss the situation and come up with a course of action. In some cases, if dispersal is not being used as a tactic to prevent the power structure from estimating the strength of the organization, a meeting might then be held of the entire membership for discussion and approval of a final plan of action.

This process will be of great value in convincing members of the poor people's organization of their own individual importance to the organization and will help give them a sense of their own dignity and worth. Too often poor people are used and manipulated in power struggles. Eventually many of them develop the feeling that their own ideas and opinions are of little value. In mass meetings, the discussion is dominated by the more vocal members, who often do not really represent and speak for the general membership. Breaking discussion down into groups of six or eight gives those who are unaccustomed to or afraid of speaking in public the chance to express their own thoughts and feelings. By doing so, they develop a sense of being a part of the organization. They feel they are valued for who they are and that their views are also important. The dignity that comes from self-esteem is one of the most important tools the organizer can give to poor people. Belief in one's own dignity as a woman or a man is one of the strongest motivating factors; from it comes the refusal to be used or abused, the assertion that "I been pushed around too long, and I ain't gonna be pushed around no more."

The way in which the organizer or the people working with him conduct these meetings will have a lot to do with how successfully those poor people who have become accustomed to silence can be drawn out. When possible, these meetings should be held in an informal atmosphere, in a place where people feel comfortable and relaxed. Often someone's home will be a good place. Sometimes it helps to serve soft drinks or coffee or to start off with a movie or tape so that people have a chance to relax. A sense of privacy and mutual trust is a must. People in the meeting must feel that they can speak freely and without fear of what they say being reported back to the power structure. The organizer should make a deliberate effort to give each member of the group a chance to speak, without pushing anyone too hard to do so. At the end of the meeting, the group should come to some sort of decision as to what it wants its representatives to say to the steering committee. If the people feel that their representatives listen to them as well as talk to them, they will eventually develop trust in them, as well as in their own ability to make decisions.

As much as possible, parliamentary procedure should be avoided. The use of parliamentary procedure creates a formal atmosphere that tends to inhibit discussion. The tactics of *Robert's Rules of Order* are in themselves power tactics, designed to limit debate and cut off minority expression of opinion. An exchange such as "Chairperson, I hereby move the previous question"; "All in favor of the previous question signify by the usual sign"; "Like sign"; or "The question is hereby approved as stated" does not provide a real opportunity for people who are not used to this way of doing business to understand what is involved or at stake. Decisions should be arrived at by discussion, with each person in the room given the chance to express his or her opinion. The group will not always arrive at a consensus, but at least those with conflicting opinions will have a chance to understand the reasoning of the other factions and to develop a feel for what is actually involved in the discussion. (Needless to say, the organizer and at least a few key leaders must have a thorough knowledge of *Robert's Rules of Order* for those situations in which poor people are forced to use parliamentary tactics in confrontations with the power structure.)

Leadership within a poor people's organization should at first be as informal as possible. It is often a good idea to rotate the chair position from meeting to meeting. This may be necessary to prevent one or two individuals from usurping leadership positions within the organization. If permanent leadership positions—president, chair, and so on—are created early in the organization's existence, they will probably be filled by the established leaders of the poor in the community. Such leaders, as noted above, will usually be loyal to the power structure rather than to the poor community. However, until the poor people in the organization have come to understand the role of these leaders and have gained confidence in their own abilities, they will tend to elect them to key positions in the organization. One of the most destructive and persistent legacies of the paternalism that exists in almost every poor community is the destruction of poor people's faith in themselves and their own abilities. Having been taught from childhood that they are not capable of thinking, speaking, or acting for themselves and must depend on leaders chosen by the power structure to think, speak, and act for them, many poor people are at first reluctant to assume positions of leadership, particularly because doing so will often expose them and their families to reprisals from the power structure. It is therefore necessary to keep these positions open until poor people are ready to step into them. The structure of the poor people's organization should be kept loose until poor people have had the time and experience to develop leadership abilities of their own.

By rotating and diversifying leadership, the organization can also help prevent the power structure from applying pressure to one or more individuals or trying to buy them off. The list of important poor people's leaders who have been fired, evicted, beaten, jailed, shot at, dynamited, and killed is tragically long. Power structures have generally accepted the same paternalistic doctrine they have attempted to teach poor people, that poor people are incapable of acting on their own behalf. As a result they firmly believe that poor people—"our poor people"—will not act for themselves. Consequently, when poor people in a community do begin to think freely, talk openly, and act decisively, the power structure psychologically rejects the idea that they are doing this on their own. Conditioned by years of manipulating poor people themselves, the members of the power structure assume that the poor people are now being manipulated by someone else for other ends. Their natural tendency is thus to look for the "agitator," "outsider," or "troublemaker" who is "stirring up the poor folks" and to try to neutralize or eliminate her, on the assumption that once she is gone, poor people will go back to behaving "like they used to."

Because of this same reasoning, power structures will often hold off making concessions to poor people's organizations while they look for ways to get rid of what they consider the source of the trouble. To be effective, a poor people's organization must move to convince the power structure that it is in reality independent; that it really represents the mass of the local poor people; that its demands are legitimately those of the poor community; that it will back its demands with action; and that it must be dealt with directly. One way of doing this is by broadening the leadership of the organization as much as possible. If a different person serves as chair at each meeting or as spokesperson for the group at each encounter, it will be difficult for the power structure to focus its attention on any one person as "the cause of the trouble." Similarly, if a group of 10 members of the poor people's organization goes to visit the mayor and the mayor asks, "Who is your spokesperson?" a good answer is, "No one; each of us speaks for everyone." One group of poor people actually went into an encounter wearing paper bags over their heads, both to dramatize the facelessness of the poor in this society and to emphasize their unity as a group.

Frequently, the power structure will attempt to weaken the organization by breaking down the unity of the leadership group. A typical approach is, "We're willing to talk to you, but we can't allow more than three people in the office at once." "We approve of what you're doing; we just don't like the leaders you've chosen to follow" is a common statement. When setting up a committee on which representation of the poor is required, the power structure will often give representation to the poor people's organization but insist on choosing the organization's representatives. All tactics of this type must be resisted strongly. Poor people's organizations must insist on the right to choose their own representatives and spokespeople, on their right to meet openly with the power structure, and on their right to send as few or as many representatives as they feel effective to such meetings, as well as to decide which of these representatives will speak for the poor people.

It should be obvious that, for many reasons, the organizer can never assume a position as leader or spokesperson within a poor people's organization. If she does so, she reinforces the power structure's ideas about the nature of poor people and reduces the probability that they will deal on a direct and realistic basis with the organization. By occupying a leadership position, she prevents poor people from moving into that position and gaining the experience necessary to eventually fill it effectively. She increases the dependence of the organization on her and makes her eventual withdrawal from the community more difficult and precarious. She also opens herself up to pressure and retaliatory measures. In recent years there has been a sharp increase in attempts to silence organizers; a large number of extremely good organizers are in such physical danger or under such extreme pressure that they can no longer operate effectively in their communities. The need for good organizers is so great in terms of the total struggle for the rights of the poor that the organizer cannot afford to risk herself unnecessarily. This is not to say that risks will not be present or that they should not be taken, but situations in which there is a high degree of personal risk should not be deliberately sought out if they can be avoided.

It is also important for the organizer to resist attempts by the power structure to deal with her directly rather than with the poor people's organization. Organizers, especially those from middle-class backgrounds, are often approached along these lines: ''Look, you're intelligent, you're educated, you can talk our language. We want to help these people, but they just don't understand the way things have to be done. If we can sit down with you privately, we can work these things out.'' Many organizers find it hard to resist such a strong appeal to their egos. To attempt to work in this way, however, could be severely damaging to the development of the poor people's organization. The organizer must always remember that eventually she must leave the community and that whatever roles she fills will be vacated when she leaves. Her responsibility is not to be a leader of the poor, but to work with the poor community while it develops leaders of its own; not to be a spokesperson for the poor, but to help them speak for themselves.

To accomplish these goals, the organizer must at all times minimize the dependence the poor community and the poor people's organization have on her. She should never, for example, chair a meeting of poor people or take a major part in the discussions. If asked for advice, she should respond briefly; if she feels that the discussion is going well, she can simply say she doesn't have anything to add to it. As soon as possible, she should begin excusing herself from meetings, so that poor people have a chance to develop skills and experience without feeling dependence on her. By careful use of such tactics, the organizer can begin to prepare the community for her eventual withdrawal, so that her departure will not come as a traumatic shock.

Such tactics may be personally very difficult for the organizer. Most good organizers rapidly become minor heroes in the communities they are working in. People identify with them, depend on them, and in many cases attribute their success to them. Such idolization of the organizer, however, works against the goal of achieving community self-confidence and self-reliance. No matter how personally satisfying it may be, the organizer must never become the center of attention. He should never become a part of the organization or of the community; he must always maintain a certain distance. There will be many situations in which the organizer could speed up the progress of the organization by assuming a leadership role—for example, by taking a group of poor people to the county commissioner's office or to the welfare department. However, he should refuse to give in to the temptation to lead poor people himself and work toward the point where the organization is self-sufficient and independent enough to move on its own. If a poor people's organization is not yet ready to take action without the organizer, it is not yet ready to take action at all.

 Chapter 7

Setting Priorities

Once the organizer has brought members of the poor community together in an organization, she must begin working with them to analyze the problems that affect the lives of poor people in the area and to help them set priorities for the organization. This analysis will involve identification of the problems of the poor community; ranking of the problems in the order of their importance to the people there; developing strategies that could be used to deal with each of the problems; evaluating the effectiveness of each of these strategies; evaluating the effect of each of these strategies on the development of the poor people's organization; and selecting those problems and strategies that will be given priority.

Using their personal knowledge of the area, as well as statistical information, the organizer and the people she is working with should compile an objective profile of the area's problems. The following set of questions, while not complete, is typical of the kinds of questions that should be asked. For convenience, it is broken down by general problem areas.

Employment

♦ Are enough jobs available for those who want to work? Do these jobs pay above minimum wage? Do they pay minimum wage only?

Do they pay below minimum wage? Are working conditions good enough to make these jobs attractive?

◆ Are opportunities for employment, equal wages, and promotion available to ethnic groups? To women? To older workers? To teenagers? To people who are developmentally disabled or physically handicapped? To people with AIDS?

◆ Is transportation to jobs available for those in rural areas? For those in the inner city?

◆ Are day care facilities available so that parents with young children can work?

◆ Is the skill level of those without jobs high enough for the jobs that are open? If not, is training available?

Housing

◆ How many people are living in substandard homes? In homes without electricity? In homes without a safe water supply? In homes with outdoor toilets? In homes with asbestos or lead-based paint?

◆ How many of these homes are rented? Are the rents fair? Are they collected honestly? Are people evicted summarily? Are necessary repairs being made?

◆ How many people live in public housing projects? How many vacancies are available? Are the rents reasonable? Are people in the projects treated fairly? Are they given adequate notice before eviction? Are they evicted without cause? Are apartments entered without notice to tenants? Are necessary repairs made? Are there recreational facilities? Day care facilities? Are social services available? Do tenants have a voice in the operation of the project?

◆ Are there houses available for poor people who want to buy homes? Are loans available for poor people who want to build homes? Is land available for sale to poor people who want to build homes?

Health

◆ Is medical care available free to those who can't afford to pay? Is this treatment easily available? Are clinic patients treated with respect?

- Are Medicare and Medicaid patients accepted by local doctors? Are they given the same treatment as other patients?

- Are opportunities for birth control available? Are they available free?

- Are immunizations given free to those who want or need them?

- Are nursing homes and old-age homes available free to those who need them?

- Is an effort being made to control rats? To collect garbage? To dispose of sewage?

- Are people with addictions to alcohol and other drugs harassed? Are they given real opportunities for treatment?

- Are there clinics for expectant mothers? Are babies delivered at home? By midwives? Are free hospital deliveries available to those who can't pay? Is the infant mortality rate too high?

- Do the schools have classes for persons who are developmentally or physically disabled or blind?

- Are psychological services available for those who need them?

- Are medical treatment and support services available to people with AIDS?

Public Services

- Are streets paved? Are there sidewalks? Are water, gas, and sewer lines available? Are there stop signs, stop lights, and street signs in poor neighborhoods?

- Are housing and building codes enforced? Are unsafe buildings condemned and torn down? Is rent control in effect? Is it enforced? Do zoning regulations discriminate against poor people?

- Is police protection available in poor neighborhoods? Do the police discriminate against poor people and ethnic groups? Against lesbians and gay people? Against people with disabilities?

- Is fire protection available? Does the fire department respond as quickly to calls from poor people as to other calls?

- Are recreational facilities available? Are they in poor neighborhoods? Is recreation supervised?

- Are poor people treated fairly by the courts? Is legal aid available to those who can't pay? Is legal advice available free? Are conditions in

jails good? Do court social workers help parolees? Do poor people
get to sit on juries?

◆ Are poor people receiving all the services they are entitled to from
such agencies as the welfare department, social security, the
Veterans Administration, the public health department, employment
offices, vocational rehabilitation agencies, and the local community
action agency? Are they treated with respect by people in these
agencies? Are they addressed by courtesy titles (Mr. or Ms.)? Are
their homes entered without notice? Are they cut off arbitrarily from
public assistance? Are they informed of their rights of appeal? Are
poor people employed by these agencies? Are these agencies located
in places where poor people can get to them easily? Do poor people
have a voice in the planning and conduct of these agencies?

Education

◆ Are schools responsive to the needs of poor people? Do they teach
ethnic group history? Do poor people and ethnic group members
have teaching jobs? In all schools? Are teachers employed according
to their qualifications? Are administrators hired and promoted the
same way?

◆ Are there vocational education classes? Adult basic education
classes? General equivalency diploma classes? Classes for school
dropouts?

◆ Do the schools help poor students get scholarships to college? Do
they help poor students get good jobs after graduation? Are there
classes for students with learning disabilities? Are special services
(speech, psychological) provided? Are health services given to all
students? Do teachers work in the homes of their students? Are sex
education and information on birth control provided?

◆ Do poor people have a voice in the determination of school policies?
Do poor people sit on the school board?

Consumer Affairs

◆ Are stores located in areas where they are accessible to poor people?
Are prices higher in these stores than in other stores? Is the quality
of goods lower than in other areas?

◆ Is credit available to poor people? Are credit rates comparable to those in other areas? Are accurate records kept? Are goods arbitrarily repossessed? Are people's wages garnisheed? Do they lose their jobs because of garnishment? Are consumer protection laws enforced?

Organization of the Poor

◆ Are poor people organized into groups that are effective in making their needs known? Are these groups successful in getting their demands met?

◆ Are the traditional spokespeople for poor people representative of them? Do they express directly the real needs and demands of the poor?

◆ Do the poor people's organizations have broad support in the poor community? Are they open to all poor people? Do the members have a voice in deciding policy?

◆ Are poor people effectively represented at the decision-making level in the community? Are they able to elect their own representatives to public office?

Complete and accurate answers to these questions and others will assist the organizer in making a comprehensive, objective profile of the problems in the community. More important, though, is the way the poor themselves see these problems in terms of their own lives. Understanding how the poor community sees these problems is the key to developing an effective strategy for the community. Often the problems that seem to be the most pressing are not those about which poor people in the community are most deeply concerned. On the other hand, the problems that are of vital importance to poor people themselves may appear to be relatively minor. In any case, the felt needs of the poor must take precedence over anything else, especially the organizer's own idea as to which problems are the most important. Otherwise, attempts to deal with the problems will lack the emotional identification by the poor that is the key to a successful strategy.

For example, on the basis of his analysis of the community's objective needs, the organizer may decide that jobs and houses are needed more than anything else. The people in the community may feel most strongly about abuses by the police. If the organizer attempts to push his priorities onto the people, they will not identify with or involve themselves in the poor people's organization. But if the organizer and the people he is working with try to deal with the problems that most concern the community, people in the community will identify and work with the organization.

The next step is to develop strategies to deal with these problems. Not all the problems of a community can be solved with the same ease or in the same length of time. Many strategies require a high degree of development of the poor people's organization and considerable experience on the part of its members. Another question is whether the support and cooperation of the power structure could be gained and whether this would be helpful or harmful. Sometimes the open opposition of the power structure actually helps build the strength of the poor people's organization. In any event, it is important that the organization's first attempt be a success, to build support for the organization among poor people. Many poor people share an attitude of defeatism, a feeling that nothing can happen in their community that can change the way they live for the better. If the organization's first try at forcing a change is a failure, the poor people's attitude of defeatism will be reinforced, and it will be that much harder to involve them in what the organization is trying to do.

As an example of how this process works, suppose that the organization has analyzed the problems of the community and has decided that the most important needs are housing, jobs for young people, and recreation. The poor people seem to feel most strongly about housing, jobs for young people, and the way they are treated by the welfare department. The organizer then sits down with the people in the organization and helps them understand the possible courses of action and the probable results of each. These could be summarized like this:

Problem—Housing

Most people in the community live in rented houses. Many of the houses are falling apart. Only a few have indoor toilets or hot water. All are heated by wood or coal stoves. The rental office closes at noon on the day the workers are paid at the mill; because the tenants can't possibly pay their rent on time, a late charge is added on. Rents are raised often and without reason; several families have been evicted even though their rent was paid up. Repairs are never made. Three houses burned to the ground in the past year; several children were killed. Almost all these houses are owned by one man, who also controls the bank and the mill and owns most of the vacant land in and around town. The public housing units, which are considered above average, are full, although the city has more units under construction or planned.

Strategy: One would be to force the slumlord either to bring his houses up to standard—which would be almost impossible in their condition—or to tear them down. But because of the power he has in the community, either would mean bringing tremendous pressure to bear on him, possibly in the form of a rent strike. However, he has more than 100 houses, and the poor people's organization is still small—fewer than 20 members, of whom 10 live in the slumlord's houses. Because of the counterpressure that the slumlord can bring to bear—foreclosure of notes at the bank, firings at the mill, evictions—most of his tenants would not be willing to run the risk of withholding their rent. A campaign by the poor people's organization against the slumlord could be broken fairly easily, and such a defeat would discourage other people from coming into the organization.

A second possible strategy would be for the organization to build its own houses. However, because the slumlord controls the bank, credit would not be available locally. Land would also have to be bought far outside the city limits. Financing would have to be obtained through federal programs, which would mean that construction couldn't start for several years. During this time, most people in the organization would probably become restless and start to drift away. Other people in the community, not seeing any concrete results, would not see any reason to become involved with the organization. The fairly technical work of preparing an application to a federal agency would not give much opportunity to involve the members of the organization.

In this situation, even though housing is a problem and even though the poor people feel strongly about it, a decision to take this on as the organization's first project would be wrong. The first strategy could result in the defeat of the organization and the alienation of potential members. The second involves too long a wait before any results could be seen and not enough opportunity to involve members of the organization and other people in the community.

Problem—Welfare

The welfare department has a long history of abuses against poor people. Many people eligible for benefits have been denied them. Others have been cut off without warning and have been denied the right of appeal. Caseworkers have entered homes of welfare recipients without warning and late at night. Applicants are treated rudely and called by their first names.

Strategy: To change this situation, pressure would have to be brought directly or indirectly on the welfare department. A picket line could, for example, be thrown around the welfare office. The welfare department, though, has proved insensitive to criticism in the past and would probably ignore the picket line. There is also some question whether the organization has enough strength to maintain the picket line, because most of its members, who do not draw welfare, are at work the hours the department is open.

Indirect pressure could be brought through pressure on the county commissioners, who pay a part of the annual budget and approve the choice of the welfare director. However, the commissioners have just been reelected by a large majority, and the next election is almost four years off. Besides, many of the poor people in the community are not yet registered to vote. A political threat would probably not be taken seriously at this point.

On the other hand, members of the organization have been quietly taking affidavits from persons who have been abused by the welfare department. A legal aid lawyer in a nearby city has offered to file suit against it when enough affidavits have been collected, but this will probably take some time. In this situation, where a long-range strategy shows good promise of real results and where the available short-range strategies are not very promising, it is best to avoid making an immediate confrontation and to continue laying the groundwork for a more successful confrontation later on.

Problem—Recreation

There are no recreational facilities whatsoever in the poor neighborhoods. Young children play in the streets and are occasionally hit by passing cars. Older children hang out at the pool halls and bars and are often arrested after fights and shootings.

Strategy: In talking with the organizer, the mayor has mentioned her concern over the lack of recreational facilities for poor children. She has said that if a representative group from the poor community would come to see her and ask for recreational facilities, she would support them and ask for funds from next year's budget.

People in the community, though, are not especially concerned by the lack of recreation. They have also said that they are tired of having to go beg the mayor for anything they want and that the city should do what is right with their tax money without having to be asked. If the organization did send a group to see the mayor, many people in the poor community would feel they were playing along with the power structure. Their attitude is, "If the mayor wants to do it, she should either do it or shut up." In this situation, even though the problem is one the organizer feels should have priority and even though there is a strategy that could solve the objective problem in a short time, the feelings of the poor people about relations between their community and the mayor and their lack of emotional feeling about the problem would make this a poor strategy to follow.

Problem—Jobs for Young People

Few summer jobs exist for young people in the community. What jobs there are go to friends of the businesspeople and merchants. Poor students spend the summer looking for things to do, and many of them wind up in trouble.

Strategy: Last summer, there were a few incidents that looked as if they could turn into a riot. The power structure is uneasy about the situation and is looking for ways to "cool it." The young people in town are angry about the lack of jobs and have often talked of doing something about it. The organizer has talked to a number of them about going in groups of three or four to negotiate with the merchants about summer jobs and has offered to train them to do it. The response has been enthusiastic. Many of the parents are also concerned about the lack of jobs and believe it leads their children to leave home after graduation from high school or to drop out early.

In this situation, there is an issue that is both pressing when looked at objectively and an object of real concern and anger in the poor community. There are enough young people involved in the organization to carry out the strategy of negotiating with the merchants. The young people in the community, who are the ones most directly affected by the problem, are also those most likely to take stronger action if the negotiations fail to produce results. Because most of them have little else to do during the summer anyway, they could easily be involved in a pressure campaign to produce jobs. In view of the city's concern over a potentially volatile situation, the merchants might actually come up with some good jobs. If so, the organization will have won an important victory. If not, the organization will have an issue with broad community support to base further action around. Because this strategy seems most likely to lead to success, the problem of jobs for young people should be selected as the target for the organization's first move.

The above examples are only indications of a process that must be gone through in great detail. In an actual organizing situation, many more problems and strategies would be examined in depth. How successful the organizer will be in helping the poor people through this process will depend on how well he has done his earlier analyses of the community, its problems, and its resources. More important will be his understanding of the attitudes of the poor community toward the different problems and strategies. The organizer who has a good understanding of the way poor people in the community feel and react toward different situations will be able to help them develop effective strategies. The effectiveness of these strategies will be judged by the way they help in solving short-range problems and by how well they help the organization build up its strength to take on more difficult projects, especially those that depend on broad community involvement and support.

 Chapter 8

Power Tactics

Many of the strategies that poor people's organizations will use have as their goal persuading or forcing the power structure in their community to meet certain of their needs. Before putting such strategies into effect, the organization must decide whether the problems in question can realistically be solved by action on the part of the power structure as it now exists in their community. This in turn will depend on whether the power structure is willing—or can be forced—to deal with the problem and whether it would in fact be able to do so in view of the resources available to it.

Generally, the things that a power structure is willing to do for poor people, it is already doing or will do with a little persuasion from the poor people—that is, if "asked politely." No poor people's organization, though, is about to go through the bowing and scraping that comes under most power structure definitions of politeness. Most power structures, in turn, will view a direct and open request from the poor community as pressure, and because of the paternalistic tradition in most poor communities, as soon as any pressure is applied to the power structure, it loses its willingness to make any concessions whatsoever. At this point, pressure must be increased to where the power structure *must* make the concessions demanded. In the extreme extension of this case, a poor people's organization will put pressure on a power structure to do something that it knows the power structure cannot do, to force a confrontation and polarize the community, as a prelude to consolidating and increasing the power of the poor community itself.

Once the poor people's organization has decided that the power structure cannot be asked or persuaded successfully to meet its demands, or when it has decided for other reasons that it does not want to use these channels, it must begin the process of applying pressure to the power structure. The general strategy for forcing a power structure to do something it is able but not willing to do consists of a series of escalating steps, proceeding from the least pressure the poor people's organization can bring to bear on the power structure to the greatest. Occasionally this entire process is reversed, and the full weight of the poor people's organization is thrown behind an issue that is relatively minor. The reasoning behind this tactic is that power structures are accustomed to rationality, the proportioning of means to ends, and when the means are totally out of proportion to the ends, they are thrown off balance. Like the tactic of trying to force the power structure to do something it is not capable of doing, this tactic is used to force a confrontation. In most situations, however, the applying of pressure proceeds in regular steps from least to most.

Before initiating a campaign of this type, it is necessary to analyze the distribution of authority and the decision-making process within the power structure as it relates to the problem that concerns the poor people, to determine the points to apply pressure. As an example, say that the poor people's organization has focused on conditions in the local housing project as its first priority. In its analysis of the problems of the community, these conditions—exorbitant rents, summary evictions, disrespect for tenants, unwarranted additional charges, entry of apartments without notice to tenants—were, on an objective basis, rated among the most serious in the community. They were also the problem about which poor people in the community—many of whom, though not now living in the projects, were formerly tenants—felt most strongly. The organization knows that changes in the operation of the projects are well within the capabilities of the power structure. There is no reason why rents cannot be lowered, why due process cannot be used in eviction cases, why tenants cannot be treated courteously, why additional charges cannot be limited to those that are necesary and reasonable, or why tenants cannot be notified before apartments are entered—except the unwillingness of the power structure to do so.

An analysis of the decision-making authority within the power structure as it relates to the housing projects might go as follows:

- The projects are administered by a salaried director.
- The director is appointed by a five-person public housing authority board.
- Members of the public housing authority board are appointed by the mayor and approved by the city council.
- The mayor is elected annually, as are members of the city council. Generally, they are members of and represent the interests of the business community.

In evaluating the vulnerability of each of these levels of authority, it is important to distinguish between the power exercised *through a position* and the power exercised *by the person occupying that position*. For example, a mayor may exercise tremendous leverage within a community as a result of backing by business and industry but be a relatively poor and powerless person. Such people are often chosen by the power structure as figureheads. Most sophisticated power structure members, like most good organizers, prefer to maintain a background position. On the other hand, a person in a relatively minor position, say a school board member, may have tremendous power because of personal wealth and control within the community. In the above example, analysis might show that the housing director had important links with other power structure members in the community and tended to act independently and with authority; that the members of the public housing authority board tended to come from outside the centers of power in the community, were appointed to the board because of their lack of assertiveness, and rubber-stamped whatever the housing director did; and that the mayor, while acting to a degree independently, tended to carry out what the business and industrial leaders in the community felt was in their own interest.

A preliminary prediction based on this analysis would suggest that ultimately pressure would have to be brought directly on the business community itself. A number of steps, however, could precede this:

- The poor people's organization requests an interview for five of its representatives with the housing director. At the interview, they present their grievances. The director states that he does not have the authority to make changes without the authorization of the board.

- The organization requests an interview with the public housing authority board. The board states that it has confidence in its director and sees no need to make any changes in the operation of the projects.

- The organization requests an interview with the mayor. At the interview, the mayor states that he is in sympathy with their demands but cannot act without authorization from the city council.

- The organization requests an interview with the city council. A press story on the day following the meeting quotes the council as saying that it has investigated the charges made by the poor people's organization and found them without basis and that it further does not feel that the representatives from the poor people's organization are truly representative of the tenants in the housing projects.

- The poor people's organization releases to the state press signed affidavits from housing project tenants documenting conditions, which are published in a lead story, in the hopes of gaining support within the local community. The community, however, reacts defensively, terming the demands "unreasonable" and the representatives of the poor people's organization "irresponsible."

- Members of the poor people's organization meet privately with some leading members of the business community and inform them that unless conditions at the projects are changed, a boycott of the downtown stores will be called. The businesspeople state that the operation of the projects is the responsibility of the public housing authority and that there is nothing they can do.

- The poor people's organization calls a boycott.

The above progression is, in outline, one that has taken place in many communities where an emerging poor people's organization has come to grips for the first time with a power structure unaccustomed to such tactics. The progression essentially follows "the rules of the game" as it is supposed to be played. An experienced poor people's organization or a power structure accustomed to dealing with such an organization would have broken the rules at any of a number of points. For example, after the initial meeting with the housing director, the power structure, recognizing that the demands cost it nothing, could have instituted the requested changes, thus robbing the poor people's organization of its issue and forcing it to develop a whole new strategy. The poor people's organization could counter this move by refusing to accept the concessions unless other, additional demands were met—thus raising the ante and protecting its strategy. The power structure's counter to this move might be to announce some concession other than those demanded by the organization, such as a new recreation center in the poor community, which might swing some public opinion in the poor community to the side of the power structure and at the same time protect its image in the rest of the community by appearing not to yield to the demands of the poor people's organization. Another power structure move at this point might be to raise the ante again by declaring the poor people's organization to be subversive, communist controlled, and a threat to the community and firing all public employees who associated with it.

When an experienced poor people's organization confronts an experienced power structure, the preliminaries are often passed over quickly, and the struggle moves rapidly into the power arena, the move/countermove situation suggested above. In the end, the strategy chosen by either side reflects more than anything else its estimate of the potential power of the other side in relation to its own. In the words of more than one organizer, "Power is where it's at." The organizer in this situation must serve as a tactician skilled in the use of power tactics if he is to be effective in helping the poor people in the community achieve their goals.

Often one of the strongest things that an organizer has going for him, especially in the South, is the myth of federal intervention. Many people view the federal government as watching every move they make and ready to file suit against them if they make a mistake. Actually, federal control at the local level, with the possible exception of education, is pathetically minimal. Most welfare-type agencies have been in existence since the days of the New Deal and have gradually been absorbed within the local political structure to the point where they are now almost out of the federal orbit of control. This is particularly true of local welfare departments, Farmers Home Administration offices, U.S. Department of Labor offices, and public housing authorities. Most of these agencies, although federal in origin and funding, have over the years developed the idea that they are autonomous in authority and that their first loyalty is to the local and state power structures. The federal government has, for the most part, been content to allow these agencies to operate pretty much as they wanted to. The abuses that have resulted from this system have been extremely well documented: welfare checks cut off, food stamps withdrawn, loans denied, segregated job lists maintained, summary evictions made, exorbitant rents charged, cotton and tobacco allotments slashed. In many areas of the South it is common knowledge that failure to walk right, talk right, act right, and vote right is sufficient grounds for any of the above. Moreover, many local power structures have come to view such punitive action not as any violation of federal law, but as their inalienable right.

On the other hand, most of the heads of these agencies share in the federal-intervention myth. They are aware that in responding to local political pressure, they are also violating the rules of their own departments. It is common practice for such agencies to make up their regulations as they go along. Applicants for welfare benefits will be told, "It's against regulations"; "We'd like to help you, but we're not allowed to"; "The government won't permit us to do it." Very few poor people, in such a situation, are going to ask to see the specific regulation under which they are being turned down.

Consequently, the organizer who has an in-depth knowledge of the regulations of a particular department is in a position to exert tremendous pressure on it. When, for example, the organizer accompanies a welfare recipient to the welfare office and they are told the application has been turned down because "you're making too much money," if the organizer can say (correctly), "I believe that in this state the ceiling for a family of four is $435," he is in effect serving notice on the welfare department that he knows it is violating its own regulations. Many departments, faced with the knowledge that they are in violation of the law and that the organizer knows it and can document it, will begin straightening up, at least for cases they feel are connected with the organizer. One thing that helps the organizer here is that very few people have a sophisticated understanding of the ins and outs of the federal bureaucracy. Anyone coming into an area from the outside, with the vaguest links to the federal government, will popularly be attributed much more power and influence with "the feds" than he actually has. When using power tactics, it is just as well not to dispel this illusion.

Obtaining copies of departmental regulations often calls for considerable creativity on the part of the organizer. Sometimes other poor people's organizations in the state will have copies—regulations in most cases will vary from state to state. A sympathetic welfare worker in another county might be able to let the organizer borrow a copy of the state regulations long enough to copy them. Or a college professor might be able to request copies of regulations from the state department for "research"—which they would certainly be used for. Of course, such regulations are legally public information, but getting to see them is another matter. If all else fails, a legal aid lawyer armed with a copy of the Federal Freedom of Information Act might work. However he gets them, the organizer should have available regulations of all public agencies he comes in contact with, so that he can develop effective tactics to be used in dealing with them and so that he can train members of the poor people's organization in the use of the same tactics.

One of the most important tools in dealing with public agencies is extensive and accurate documentation. Documentation can serve as a basis for administrative appeal, for legal action, or for pressure campaigns based on public relations. Anytime anything occurs at an agency that might later be useful, the organizer and the poor person she went with should each make out a brief statement of what happened. These should be short and to the point. For example,

> On May 23, 1969, I went to the Welfare to see could I get on. The lady at the desk told me I was too old, and why didn't I get me a job working in the peach orchard. I said well I'd like to apply anyway but she said no and told me to get out and go on home.
>
> William F. Jones

> On May 23, 1969, I accompanied Mr. William F. Jones to the offices of the Lindsey County Welfare Department in Centerville. The lady at the front desk, Ms. Walters, said, "Why, William, you're too old to apply. Why don't you go over to Perkins and get a job picking peaches?" Mr. Jones said, "Well, I'd like to put one in anyway." Ms. Walters answered, "I'm afraid I can't let you do that, William, it would be against regulations. Now you and your friend go on home and let me get my work done."
>
> Edna Varner

These statements can later be sworn to before a notary and converted into affidavits if necessary. Needless to say, they should be kept in a safe place, preferably out of the area, and the fact that they are being collected should be publicized as little as possible. For a small fee, the organizer and one or two key members of the poor people's organization can have themselves appointed notaries, which can be very useful when documents are being prepared that need to be kept confidential.

Almost all public agencies grant applicants a right of appeal, and this right should be used to the full extent. Anytime an applicant for welfare, social security, Farmers Home Administration loans, Small Business Administration loans, food stamps, surplus commodities, veterans' benefits, or the like is turned down, an appeal should be filed unless it is absolutely certain that the applicant is really ineligible. In most cases, the applicant can simply write a brief statement such as "I, William F. Jones, wish to appeal the decision denying me welfare benefits," sign his or her name, and send it to the appropriate agency. A copy should be kept, and the letter should be sent certified mail (cheaper than registered), return receipt requested, so that the applicant will have proof of receipt by the agency. The organizer should, of course, research the regulations of the department to be sure the rules for filing appeals are followed, to avoid having appeals turned down for "failure to seek administrative relief in accordance with regulations."

The decision to begin an intensive appeals campaign against an agency is basically a strategic decision. Before deciding to initiate such a campaign, the organizer and the people she is working with should make sure that the people being turned down by the agency actually have legitimate grounds for appeal. Often people who are in severe need of help, who should be entitled to benefits in any humane welfare system, are legally excluded from such benefits. For example, an unemployed widow whose children are over 18 is legally excluded from benefits from the welfare or any other federal program unless she can prove that she is "totally and permanently disabled," a condition defined by Congress as incapable of holding any job that exists anywhere in the United States, whether or not such a job actually exists in her county or state, whether or not vacancies exist in such jobs, and whether or not she could be hired if she applied. In many cases, when people feel they have been turned down illegally, the welfare department is only following the restrictive and repressive regulations enacted by Congress.

The success of a pressure campaign based on appeals will depend in large measure on the legitimacy of these appeals. If, for example, a state welfare department receives in a month 30 appeals against one county welfare department and 28 of the appeals are upheld, pressure will probably be brought on the county by the state to straighten up and stop using so much state time. On the other hand, if 28 of the 30 appeals are turned down and there are legal grounds for doing so, the pressure will backfire on the organizer and the people she is working with.

In the early stages of a pressure campaign, one commonly used tactic is to create pressure on the power structure by suggesting or implying what might take place if demands are not met. Such suggestions may be made discreetly and indirectly at times; at other times they may be very direct and explicit. Generally, it is to the advantage of the poor people's organization to make such suggestions as subtly as possible, provided their meaning is communicated. When such suggestions are made directly and explicitly, most power structures will feel and react as if they were being threatened or blackmailed. One of the rules politicians follow is never to back down under pressure if possible, or, more precisely, never to back down under pressure when the pressure is publicly recognized as such. Once the nonpoor public becomes aware that the power structure is being "threatened," it will tend to close ranks behind the power structure. Consequently, pressure at this point should be as strong as possible yet as silent as reasonable. The pressure should be felt but not heard.

This tactic follows one of the general rules for dealing with power structures when the goal of the poor people's organization is to achieve concrete goals, as opposed to forcing a confrontation: Always give the power structure an out. Creative power tactics will provide a situation in which the power structure can give in to the demands of the poor people without appearing to have done so. One common tactic is for the poor people's organization to make exorbitant, unreasonable, and irrelevant demands before beginning serious negotiations with the power structure. Say, for example, that the real goal of the poor people is extension of paving and sewage lines to the poor areas of town. An initial set of "prenegotiation" demands might include removal of the police chief; impeachment of the mayor; guaranteed annual income for all city residents, paid by the city; public jobs for all unemployed people; and amnesty for all city prisoners. After a month or so of digesting such demands, many power structures will be glad to talk privately about streets and sewage.

In such a situation, it is extremely important that members of the poor people's organization understand the tactic that is being used; otherwise many of them will feel that the poor people's organization has been the loser in the struggle. The members of the organization must understand that if they are successful in achieving their goals, it is just as well if the power structure members think *they* have won—because they will be that much more willing to absorb a loss the next time around. In the above situation, for example, the power structure could pave the streets and extend sewage lines and still claim, for the purpose of holding together its constituency at election time, that it had resisted the demands of the poor and was only doing things that had been planned for a long time. In situations when the poor do not have the numerical strength to replace a power structure, it is just as well to maintain a group in power that is accustomed to making concessions.

To communicate controversial suggestions discreetly to the power structure, the organizer must develop regular and reliable channels of communication to its members. One good method is for the organizer to develop relationships with some of the persons whom the power structure uses as its own information links to the poor community. The organizer is then in a position to influence the picture of attitudes within the poor community that is relayed back to the power structure. She can, for example, mention to one of these "stools" her concern over the possible outbreak of violence if certain conditions are not changed. Most stools will be sure to relay this observation back as their own, probably reinforced by some of the things they have heard themselves. In their position, it is better to overestimate than underestimate the seriousness of a situation, because few power structures are concerned with overcontaining trouble. If a power structure can be convinced by such methods that a situation is potentially serious, it may be willing to negotiate certain concessions to cool the situation.

If a power structure cannot be convinced that a potentially serious situation exists in a poor community, whether or not such a situation does in fact exist, or if, even though convinced of the seriousness of the situation, it refuses to make any concessions, then actual direct pressure must be applied. This point is reached fairly quickly in most situations, particularly in those communities where poor people are being organized for the first time and where the power structure, because of its paternalistic background, is convinced that poor people in the community will not move on their own behalf. In many situations, especially in the civil rights movement, the next step by the poor people's organization has been what might be roughly described as "social tactics"—marches, sit-ins, mass meetings, picket lines. There was a point when such tactics were seen by the power structure as power tactics and were reacted to accordingly, usually with official violence. However, experienced power structures understand today that such tactics do not in themselves affect the real centers of power in a community. Most power structures know by now that the Alabama state patrol did more to help the civil rights movement than to hurt it, and will go out of their way to avoid being responsible for similar situations.

Social tactics are useful for two purposes: as a means of mobilizing poor people prior to taking action against the real centers of power, and as a way of notifying the power structure that this mobilization exists and can be directed in economic, political, and other ways against it. A march can be called to protest the shooting of a young student by a police officer as a way of bringing poor people together in their determination to do something about the conditions that produced the incident. But it should also be made clear to the power structure, by and through the march, that if it does not take action to deal with these incidents and the conditions that cause them, more direct measures will be taken: a boycott, a strike, self-defense measures in the poor community.

It is important to distinguish between these social tactics in themselves and the power they represent. A march called to initiate a boycott is effective only if the boycott is effective. A sit-in at a lunch counter works only if it prevents the restaurant from doing business. A picket line around a plant is important as a symbol of the strike— if it keeps workers out of the plant. A picket line around the mayor's house should be used only when it represents the intention and the ability of the people to vote her out of office. Such tactics should be used only when the organizer is confident that the poor people are actually willing and able to exercise the power these tactics symbolize. Such tactics must also be in proportion to the power at stake. If a march is called in a town of 10,000 people to kick off a boycott and only 35 people show up to march, it will do more harm to the boycott than to anything else.

Sometimes, when a power structure is convinced by such tactics that the poor community really is on the verge of initiating direct power tactics, it will move to grant the concessions the poor people are demanding. But a power structure that has been maintained in power for some time, and is therefore confident of its ability to break the back of any poor people's campaign, will be inclined to ride it out and wait for the next move. It is important to recognize that up to this point the struggle between poor people and power structure has still not moved into the real power arena and that the next move is the one that takes the struggle into the area where real power is exercised.

Real power tactics are economic, political, or violent in nature. Of these, economic tactics are probably the most relevant in most rural areas at the present time. Only a small proportion of the counties in the South, for example, have a poor white or poor black population of over 60 percent, the number that is almost necessary for a political takeover. And only in a very few rural areas are there organizing efforts that are directed at political coalitions between blacks and poor whites, between Chicanos and poor blacks, or between coalitions of other groups. Such coalitions may become more common in the near future, but at present are a realistic goal in only a few areas.

Violence has traditionally and continually been used by power structures as an instrument for achieving and maintaining power, but very few organizers are presently using violence as a way of achieving power for poor people. It is highly probable that if on a national basis the present trend toward denying the rights of the poor continues, violence will increase. Even now, this potential for violence is an important factor in power struggles. But the deliberate use of violence as an organizing tactic has not yet developed to a significant extent in this country.

Moreover, both violence and politics are essentially means to economic ends. Whatever may be the basic motivating factors of human behavior, it is a historical fact that power in this country has been sought primarily for economic ends. In the continuing debate over the psychological, educational, social, and cultural characteristics of the poor, the one factor that most distinguishes them from the nonpoor is often lost sight of: their lack of money. The other characteristics that are often attributed only to poor people are generally shared with other groups. The middle class, for example, is also effectively shut out from the real centers of power and decision making. All members of ethnic groups, not just the poor, are subjected to indecent discrimination. These groups have generally been forced to go along with these other deprivations as the price of economic success. Only the poor suffer from economic deprivation as well. The only difference between the lawyer and the office worker who both get drunk over the weekend is that the rich person can afford it and the poor person can't—and that the lawyer gets driven home by the police while the office worker spends the night in jail.

It is natural, then, that the goals of most poor people's organizations will be at base economic and that many of the tactics that are used will be economic in nature. Increasingly, economic tactics are being used to achieve general goals and in the process are being directed against the power structure in general rather than against specific and individual businesses and industries. Traditionally, economic tactics have been specific and individual. For example, if an industry was not providing decent wages and working conditions, a strike was called against that particular plant. If a business discriminated in hiring or sold inferior goods, a boycott was called against that business. Now, however, because the interlocked economic interests of the power structure have begun to be more widely recognized, such tactics are increasingly being used indirectly. For example, a boycott may be called of the downtown area to protest unfair practices by the welfare department. Such tactics not only provide an effective way of creating indirect pressure on the political arms of the power structure, they have the additional effect of dividing the power structure by setting its various elements off against each other.

It is important to recognize that power structures are rarely as unified or monolithic as they are usually considered. Quite often there will be serious conflicts of interest and divisions within the power structure. The careful use of economic tactics can exploit and intensify these conflicts to the advantage of the poor community by forcing some members of the power structure to bring pressure on others.

For example, one of the common problems in rural communities with a heavily agricultural base is that the power structure deliberately prevents new industry from moving in, to maintain the low-paid agricultural labor pool. In such a situation, a boycott may be called against the town merchants to protest the lack of industrial jobs. The merchants are thus placed in a position of being forced to offset the efforts of the agricultural members of the power structure to keep out industry—if they want their businesses to stay open. At the same time, the business community can be made aware that new industry would mean more jobs and higher wages in the community and thus more sales and larger profits. If the boycott continues to be effective, the business community, caught between loss of profits on the one hand and the possibility of greater profits on the other, may move to attract industry to the community. It might do this by providing facilities for industrial use, pooling funds to establish an industry, or persuading the county government to use public funds to construct industrial parks and facilities.

A boycott is an extremely difficult tactic to carry out effectively. In communities where a large proportion of the poor people are dependent on the power structure for employment and housing, strong counterpressure can easily be brought against them to break the boycott. In rural areas, there may also be a serious problem of getting food and supplies. If the poor people's organization is not prepared to meet these needs if necessary—by busing people to adjacent communities to shop or by setting up cooperative businesses in the community—the boycott may be broken simply because people will have no choice except to buy. A boycott also has the usual effect of increasing local buying by nonpoor residents who might normally shop in nearby urban areas, which may be sufficient to offset the effects of the boycott. If the poor people's organization does not have a high degree of membership awareness and participation to begin with, a general boycott can be almost impossible to maintain.

When selective boycott techniques are used—only one or two businesses are boycotted rather than the entire business community—other businesspeople may help out those whose stores are being boycotted, either by loans or occasionally by splitting some of their profits. Their reasoning is that if the boycott is successful at the first store or two, it will eventually move on to the other stores in town, and it is easier and cheaper to break the boycott at the start. Usually, though, the selective boycotting technique is more effective than a general boycott when the goals of the boycott involve the businesses themselves rather than general pressure on the power structure. This is especially true in rural areas where the power structure is divided and where supplying poor people while the boycott is in effect would be a problem. In this situation, the businesses to be boycotted should be chosen carefully. Some of the factors to be considered are the vulnerability of these businesses, including their ability to ride out a long boycott; their relationship to the power structure in general, including their ability to influence it when general demands are being sought, and the likelihood that other members of the power structure would help them out financially during the boycott; the emotional feelings of the poor toward each business; and its location. If a business boycotted is in the central shopping district, a picket line out front will create considerable psychological pressure on other businesspeople in the area. When possible, it is a good idea to boycott one of two similar stores within sight of each other, so that the person being boycotted can get a good look at former long-time consumers shopping across the street.

It is often useful to refer to a boycott as a "selective buying campaign." In a selective buying campaign, people are encouraged to shop at all stores except the ones being boycotted. If boycotts are illegal in the community, something the organizer should research carefully in advance, use of the term "selective buying" can avoid a court injunction against the boycott: Members of the poor people's organization can honestly say, "Why we never told people *not* to shop at Smith's." This tactic also provides good opportunities for the negotiation of demands: The poor people's organization can approach the owner of one of several grocery stores, for example, and offer to urge all its members to buy at her store if she meets their demands, such as lowering prices, giving credit, improving quality of goods, or hiring poor people in responsible positions.

It is also necessary to avoid charges of conducting a secondary boycott, which is illegal in many areas. A good example of conducting a secondary boycott is boycotting a clothing store to get the mayor to do something about police brutality. The store owner could easily get a court order against picketing and then have the pickets arrested if they continued to appear. Of course, if the poor people's organization is trying to force arrests, this is sometimes an easy way. But if not, the organization should find some issue that can be used directly against the business being boycotted, even if the real reason for the boycott is to create indirect pressure on the power structure. In the above example, the poor people's organization could state publicly that it is boycotting the clothing store because it overcharges poor folks but could make it very clear privately, through the channels it has developed to the power structure, that the real issue is the police and their conduct.

As a general rule, when the goals of the poor people's organization relate to a single business, that business alone should be boycotted. When the goals relate to the business community in general or when the boycott is used as a way of bringing indirect pressure on the power structure, a general boycott is best if it can be carried out. The decision to boycott individual businesses or the entire business community will also rest on the ability of the poor people's organization to successfully call and carry out a boycott and to resist the counterpressures on its members.

The strike as an economic tactic has been less successful than the boycott in poor communities. Most poor people who are employed work at low-paying, marginal, nonunion jobs. In such a situation, a strike has often simply produced mechanization or automation, or the industry has been able to fill its job slots with scab labor, imported or otherwise. Most employed poor people are also not covered by unemployment compensation and have no strike fund to support them while they are out of work. Consequently, the economic pressure in a poor people's strike is often harder on the strikers themselves than on the industry being struck. If a strike is called, the poor people's organization must have ways of meeting these needs—for example, by renting or purchasing buses to bring strikers to jobs in nearby cities, provided these jobs are available.

In many poor communities, the most attractive power tactic has proved to be violence. To state this is not to advocate violence as a means of achieving economic ends for poor people. However, violence is seen today by large numbers of poor people as the only possible alternative. It is not necessarily that violence has produced significant results, because in many situations the result has been entirely the opposite, but that poor people have tried all the other alternatives without success and as a consequence have become increasingly willing to try violence as a last resort. The argument that "violence will get you nowhere" is unconvincing; poor people have for years watched power structures use violence as a deliberate means to achieve and consolidate power and wealth, often with great success. The only real answer to violence is to prove that the other alternatives *can* get poor people *someplace*, to provide the resources through which poor people can achieve economic equality through nonviolent means. If this is not done, not even those organizers most committed to nonviolent progress will be able to keep the communities they work in from trying alternatives.

 Chapter 9

Building Political Power

One of the key ways in which a power structure exercises control over a community is through the political structure of that community. The elected and appointed officials of a county have tremendous power, both direct and indirect. In a time when people of many different political persuasions are concerned over the growing centralized power of the federal government, the extent to which the lives of poor people are influenced and controlled, not by the federal government, but by government at the local level, is often not recognized. In a rural county, the county government sets the tax rates, assesses property, appoints the members of the welfare board, approves the selection of the welfare director, sponsors or rejects food programs, builds roads, and appoints members of other boards and commissions. Other officials, who may be elected or appointed, run the schools, build and administer public housing, conduct health programs, register voters, select jurors, enforce the law, and run the courts. In addition, these public bodies have great discretionary power to develop new ways of meeting the needs of the people of their community, either through sponsoring federal programs available for community improvement or by using the public funds they have the authority to collect through taxes and bond issues to develop other relevant programs.

Many of the needs of poor people in a community that are not met by the programs of established agencies could be met by creative action on the part of local government. A city or county government that is truly responsive to the needs of its poor citizens could, for example, provide—

- public service jobs for poor people and use of public funds to construct industrial facilities

- enforcement of equal opportunity in employment

- transportation systems

- day care facilities, through the public school systems

- vocational training opportunities, through vocational–technical schools operated by the public school system

- comprehensive water and sewage systems

- enforcement of rent control and housing and building codes

- construction of new public housing and maintenance of fair rents and practices in existing units

- construction of new housing units, for resale at minimum interest rates

- free medical clinics, operated through the public health department, including treatment and support for people with AIDS

- enforcement of Medicare and Medicaid regulations, through action to bar doctors who violate these regulations from practicing in local hospitals

- family planning clinics, operated through the public health department

- comprehensive immunization services, operated through the public health department

- use of public funds to construct nursing and old-age homes

- rat-control projects and comprehensive garbage collection

- clinics and treatment centers for alcoholics and drug addicts

- free hospital deliveries for poor people

- classes in the school system for persons who are developmentally disabled, blind, or physically handicapped

- mental health centers offering psychological, individual, and family counseling services

- paving of all streets and roads, extension of utilities to all areas of the community, and placement of stop signs, stop lights, and street signs at all intersections

- enforcement of housing, zoning, and building regulations and rehabilitation of condemned areas through urban renewal programs funded by the federal government or in other ways

- equal police protection and law enforcement in all areas of the community and employment of poor people, ethnic group members, and women in the police department

- equal fire protection in all areas of the community and employment of poor people, ethnic group members, and women in the fire department

- construction of recreational facilities in all areas of the community and conduct of supervised recreation programs

- equal treatment of all members of the community by the courts, equal representation of poor people and ethnic groups on juries, and a system to provide legal aid and representation to those who cannot afford payment

- equal treatment of poor people by all public agencies, deliberate and aggressive efforts to ensure that all members of the community receive whatever benefits they are legally entitled to through these agencies, employment of poor people and ethnic group members in responsible positions within these agencies, and representation of poor people and ethnic groups on the boards of these agencies and on advisory committees

- aggressive programs to register all members of the community to vote

- redistricting to ensure proportionate representation of poor people and ethnic groups at all levels of government

- educational programs designed to meet the special needs of poor people, including employment of poor people and ethnic group members in teaching positions and emphasis within the curriculum on group identification, group history, and group pride

- a comprehensive system of education for adults and school dropouts

- establishment of community colleges with free tuition to provide poor people with the opportunity for advanced education

- ◆ institution of community control of schools to give poor people an effective voice in the education of their children
- ◆ enforcement of consumer protection laws
- ◆ use of public funds to provide low-cost credit to poor people
- ◆ direct discussion with poor people concerning the problems of the poor community
- ◆ recognition of members of the poor community as spokespeople for the poor
- ◆ use of public funds to provide incentive grants to poor people's organizations to assist them in developing projects of their own choosing and in broadening membership participation and education
- ◆ establishment of political education programs for poor people to assist them in electing members of the poor community to public office.

Unfortunately, no city or county in the United States has even attempted to institute a significant majority of the above points. When the above representative demands are incorporated into such broad plans as the "freedom budget" or the "poor people's campaign," they are usually termed exorbitant or unreasonable. Yet the same or equivalent programs, rights, and opportunities are enjoyed by other groups within this society. This society has never recognized poor people as first-class citizens and consequently has failed to admit that they have a right to the opportunities of first-class citizenship. The above list of options, which are legally open to any city, county, or state government, are not luxuries, but absolute necessities if poor people are to achieve equality within this society. Very few governmental groups at any level within this country have a real commitment to equality for poor people; consequently, very few take demands such as the above seriously or make a real attempt to meet them.

Many power structures are now providing or attempting to provide some of the above. In rural areas, however, even where the governing authority would be willing to provide some of these opportunities, the money to do so is simply not available. A rural county will have a limited revenue base, out of which it provides funds for schools, roads, courts, welfare, police, bond retirement, and official salaries. To meet the needs of its poor citizens, such a county would also need to construct thousands of new homes, pave miles of roads, employ hundreds of poor people in public service jobs, purchase and maintain buses for rural transportation, build and staff day care facilities, provide matching funds to build and operate a vocational school, construct countywide water and sewer systems, build and staff medical clinics and nursing and old-age homes, pay a proportion of the medical costs of the poor, build recreational facilities, construct industrial parks and facilities, expand police and fire departments, pay the costs of legal aid programs, provide funds to hire poor people in public agencies, construct and staff a community college, and pay the salaries of personnel to carry out all the above. There is no conceivable way in which such a rural county could meet this cost. Even though wealth may be grossly maldistributed within rural counties, these counties, taken as a whole, are themselves tremendously discriminated against in terms of sharing in the general prosperity of this country.

In theory, funds to provide these necessary services are provided through the federal government. In practice, the level at which funds for these purposes is expended is far below the need—perhaps less than 5 percent of what a realistic program designed to aid poor people would cost. The United States does not now have and has never had a real commitment to eliminating poverty in this society and consequently has never made available the resources to do so. In addition, there is a strong antirural bias in the distribution of those federal funds that eventually reach the poor. Nevertheless, despite these limitations, government at the local level has significant options that it can exercise if it wishes to create opportunities for poor people.

As long as the city or county government is primarily responsive to the needs of the power structure, whatever gains the poor people of the community make will be forced from the government by long, hard struggles. A much more efficient method of making the local government responsive to the needs of the poor, in those communities where it is a realistic possibility, is for the poor people to take control of all or part of the official structure. Control over a city or county government means a regular source of revenue—one of the most difficult problems that most poor people's organizations face. This revenue can be used to purchase land for housing; build hospitals, clinics, nursing homes, and training centers; purchase industrial sites and construct industrial facilities; and construct almost any other type of facility that is needed by the community. In addition, any town or county, regardless of size, is eligible for such federal programs as grants for water and sewer systems, public housing, urban renewal, and recreation areas.

It follows, then, that in those areas where it is realistic to think of gaining control of some or all elected offices—and through these, of appointed public positions—one of the organizer's key priorities will be to assist local poor people in developing the skills and knowledge necessary to build an effective political base. This means extensive work in political education, as well as in political organization. It is important to recognize that those rights of political participation that are usually taken for granted in middle-class communities—the right to register, the right to vote, the right to run for public office, the right to a secret ballot—are regarded very differently in many poor communities. The idea of the right of every citizen to vote and to have his or her vote equally represented has been a long time coming in the United States. From early laws restricting the vote to free male white property owners, through such other restrictive requirements as the "grandfather clause," literacy tests, and poll taxes, the trend has been to limit the vote to those in power and their allies. As was to be expected, power structures grew to regard control of elections as their right, rather than as a right of the people. Poor people who insisted on their right to vote or refused to allow their votes to be bought and sold were fired, evicted, run out, cut off, and shot down. There are still many areas today where to vote is to risk one's job, house, welfare, or life and where, the day after the election, the power structure knows exactly how each member of the community voted and which ones will be retaliated against for voting wrong or even for voting at all.

Inevitably, these conditions have had a strong negative effect on the willingness of poor people to participate openly in political campaigns and elections. This fear is one of the hardest obstacles the organizer has to overcome in educating poor people to participate in political power struggles. One of the strongest weapons available to combat this fear is the sense of group solidarity that comes from belonging to a well-organized, outspoken, and active poor people's organization. For this reason, it is often advantageous to begin the active work of building a political base after the poor people's organization and the people in it have gained some experience and skill in power struggles of other sorts, rather than before. Of course, an experienced organizer will lay the groundwork for eventual political organization very early in the course of her work in the community to educate poor people to the need of and possibility for political action.

Political education works best in a dynamic context. It is much easier to involve poor people in learning about registering, voting, qualifying, campaigning, poll watching, and election appealing when an actual campaign involving poor people's candidates is in operation. For the same reason, a voter registration campaign will be most effective before an election in which poor people intend to run for office. In many rural areas, poor people neglect to register and vote simply because they believe there is no one worth voting for. In many cases, there will not even be opposition candidates. When there are contests for offices, the difference between the candidates as far as poor people are concerned is often so slight as to encourage any reasonable voter to stay home or go fishing on election day.

The organizer should locate, before beginning a voter registration campaign, poor people who intend to run for office. Often the poor people's organization she works with can help in locating them and backing them as candidates. People worth voting for is a powerful lever in convincing poor people of the need to register. The candidates themselves will often prove to be the most effective registration workers. To help prevent the power structure from taking countermeasures, candidacies should not be formally announced at first, but the word can be spread quietly to motivate those who have not yet registered to do so.

The keys to a successful voter registration campaign are this emotional content—the feeling that someone will be running for office who is dedicated to making local government responsive to the needs of the poor people in the community—and extremely tight and detailed organization. Few towns or counties have such a heavy majority of poor people that potential voters can be overlooked. More elections have been lost—or stolen—by small margins than by large ones. It is important that every potential voter be located and registered.

Before beginning the actual registration campaign, the organizer and the people she is working with should become familiar with the laws and regulations governing the conduct of elections in the area. A copy of the state election code is a must. The code will provide such information as residency requirements, which will often differ for county, state, and federal elections; the number of days before an election a voter must register to be eligible to vote in that particular election; regulations concerning absentee ballots; rights of candidates to poll watchers; and procedures for demanding recounts or new elections. A detailed knowledge of these requirements can be the key to winning a close election. For example, in one state, a one-month residency is required for county elections, six months for state elections, and a year for federal elections, but white voters in at least one county have been permitted to vote in federal elections even though their residency only qualified them for county elections. Documentation of situations like this can be used to disqualify ballots, demand a recount, or request federal poll watchers. Similarly, voters who are registered just before an election may not be eligible to vote until the following election. Many poor people may attempt to vote anyway and have their ballots disqualified. Again, the regulations may require the registrar to go to the home of someone who is sick or disabled. One important point that is often overlooked is that towns and cities often have their own election codes and registration lists that are separate from the county, state, and federal codes and registration lists. Many poor people's election campaigns have been lost because the poor people, having registered for county, state, and federal elections, were under the logical impression that they could also vote in town elections, when in fact they were ineligible because they had failed to register separately.

Once the registration campaign has actually begun, the key to success is systematic work. The poor people's organization must locate every potential voter in the city or county. Sometimes various community agencies will have made detailed surveys of the area, which are in theory public information. In practice, however, it will probably be extremely difficult for a poor people's organization to obtain this information, and it is probably best if a separate survey is made. A typical survey might include the following questions:

- What are the names, ages, and birthdates of all people living in your house? Which of these are registered to vote?

- Do you have any relatives in military service? Are they registered to vote in this area?

- Do you have children or other relatives away at school? Are they registered to vote here?

- Do you have any relatives living out of the area who own land here? Are they registered to vote in the area?

- Do you have any relatives in nursing homes, hospitals, or other institutions in or out of the area? Are they registered to vote here?

- Do you have any relatives in jail for misdemeanors? Are they registered to vote?

These questions are necessary to determine which persons might be eligible to vote both by regular and absentee ballot. Most poor people's organizations register only those persons living in the county at the time the registration campaign is conducted. Many people who at the time are out of the county retain the right to vote there, depending on the regulations of the particular election code in effect in the area. Taken together, legal residents of a county who are in the military service, away at school or college, and in institutions have enough votes to swing many close elections. It is important that these people be contacted, encouraged to register, and informed of upcoming elections and candidates so that they can vote with the poor people.

It is important to determine not only which people are eligible to vote at the time the survey is taken but also those who will become eligible in time for the next election. For example, say that the voting age in a state is 18, that elections for county offices will be held on November 4, and that registration for county offices closes thirty days before an election. A file would be made of all those who will turn 18 before October 5. By checking this file, the poor people's organization can be sure it tries to register each person who might be eligible in time for an election. Separate files should be kept for those who have already registered and those who still need to register. Because such files are so important in developing a political base and because files kept by poor people's organizations often disappear, a second or even a third set should be kept in a safe location, definitely out of the county, possibly even out of the state.

A voter registration drive should be designed and conducted in such a way as to feed into the election itself. Too many instances have occurred in which large numbers of poor people registered to vote but failed to show up on election day. The registration workers should help the people they work with become aware of the upcoming election, of the candidates, of the issues involved, and of the need to vote. One of the most effective ways of educating voters is to use the same community organizing techniques used in building a poor people's organization through block organizing. If the community has already been well organized, the existing block or neighborhood organizations can take on political functions as well. The organizer working with each of these groups should also expand into the areas of voter registration and education. How openly she is able to do this will depend, of course, on the type of agency she is working for. The organizer should not become discouraged if the agency that employs her prohibits such activities—a great deal of effective voter registration and education work has been done behind the back of community action agencies and other conservative groups.

The same rules for maintaining contacts with poor people and poor people's organizations apply to political workers as to organizers. The person who visits the family to survey them for voter registration should also be the one to go with them to the registrar if necessary, to visit them from time to time to discuss the upcoming election, to bring them to community political meetings, to bring the candidates to their home and introduce them, to check with them before the election to make sure they intend to vote, to arrange for their transportation to the polls if necessary, to make sure that they vote, and to check with them afterwards to see if their rights as voters were in any way violated. These workers should also form a system of communications to provide information to the poor people. Many of the standard techniques used in political campaigns—radio spot announcements, newspaper ads, calling cards, posters, bumper stickers, buttons—have limited effectiveness in the poor community. In addition, their expense puts them out of reach of most poor people's organizations and poor people's candidates. Good political work among poor people, like good organizing, is based mostly on personal contact.

Another reason for relying on personal contact in poor people's political campaigns is to increase the relationship between the candidates and the people in their communities. This relationship should be maintained even after candidates are elected. Regular visits to poor people, block and neighborhood organizations, and larger poor people's organizations by elected poor people's officials can provide channels for the community to express its needs and for the officials to report on the progress they are making. In selecting candidates, poor people's organizations should make it clear to them that they will expect and require this type of continued contact by the officials with their constituency if they are elected.

This continued contact will also have the effect of building the political strength of the poor people's organization.

The success of the poor people's organization in politics will depend in large degree on the extent to which its political functions are well organized. This is particularly true before an election. Not only should each of the registered voters be contacted directly by the political worker from their area before the election to remind them about it and to find out if they plan to vote, but the person working with each family should also find out where they intend to vote, by what time they expect to vote at the latest, and whether transportation is needed. From this information, the poor people's organization should put together lists for each polling place with the names of all expected voters, the times they are coming to vote, who they are bringing with them, and whether they will need help in voting. Several representatives of the poor people's organization should be at the polling place to check off the voters on the list as they arrive. One or more members of the organization should also be at the polling place with cars, so that if a voter fails to arrive by the indicated time, they can be sent out to find and bring the voter in. These representatives should also have sample ballots with them so they can go over them with the voters before they enter the polling place, show them how to mark the ballot, and remind them which candidates the poor people's organization is backing. The representatives should also go over with the voters the regulations that were discussed with them earlier in individual contacts and in community meetings, including their right to go into the booth alone or to bring someone from the poor people's organization with them if they need help and their right in rural communities that still use printed paper ballots to fold the ballot and deposit it in the box without having it checked by election officials.

As the voters leave the polling place, the representatives of the poor people's organization should check with them again to make sure no voting regulations were violated. If any violations appear to have been committed, an affidavit should be taken immediately. These affidavits will be a necessity if the election is to be protested in any way or if a recount is to be demanded. They can also be instrumental in developing a request for federal poll watchers in the next election.

The same general procedures for documenting election law violations should be followed by poll watchers inside the polling places and when the votes are counted. In most areas, each candidate is entitled to two poll watchers inside the polling place and when the votes are counted. These poll watchers should make written records of violations as they occur, which can later be coordinated with the affidavits of the voters themselves. After the election, violations should be well publicized within the poor people's organization, especially if the poor people's candidates lost the election by a close margin. Knowledge that such violations occurred will help the members of the organization understand why the election was lost and will help to build motivation for the next campaign.

It should be evident that a high degree of organization and training, as well as considerable research, is necessary to successfully carry out the building of a strong poor people's political base. Political workers, polling-place attendants, runners, poll watchers, ballot-counting watchers, and affidavit takers must each be trained in their individual responsibilities. Contingency plans must be made for filing suits or following administrative procedures for recounts when violations occur in sufficient numbers to justify it. Training sessions must be held for all these persons, as well as for candidates and voters. A high degree of planning and coordination is essential.

In those areas where the poor people do not constitute a potential political majority, the same general methods are still used to develop a political base. In this situation, however, the organized voting strength of poor people is used as a lever to get concessions out of opposing candidates. The general procedure is to negotiate openly or privately with all candidates for an office for those concessions the poor people's organization has decided on. The organization then decides which candidate to back and uses the techniques outlined above to deliver votes to that candidate. If the candidate wins and the concessions are made, the poor people's organization continues to back him or her in subsequent elections unless another candidate offers more significant concessions. If the candidate backed by the poor people's organization wins the election and then fails to come through with the agreed-upon concessions, the poor people's organization automatically switches its support to another candidate in the next election. Through a series of such maneuvers, the poor people's organization will eventually establish its own power as a political force and will be able to get concessions regularly as the price of its electoral support—provided, of course, that the candidates it backs continue to win and that those it opposes continue to lose.

While these techniques have been discussed mainly in terms of town and county elections, the potential exists in several states for coalition politics based on these principles among different ethnic and racial groups. This is especially true in areas where efforts are now under way to organize separate political forces within each of these groups. The strength of poor people's political organization at the county level will eventually help determine the possibility of poor people's politics on broader state or national bases.

 Chapter 10

Self-Help Strategies

In situations where poor people and their organizations are not able to take over or significantly influence the power structure through persuasion, power tactics, or political action, the only realistic solution to their problems is self-help: programs run by and for poor people independently of the power structure. Self-help strategies will also be used in other situations: when, for example, the local power structure lacks the skills and resources to deal with a particular problem, when a program could be run better by the poor people's organization, or when self-help programs are being used as a way of building organizational strength and membership awareness before starting power or political actions.

In theory, a poor people's organization can deal with almost any problem through self-help strategies. In practice, the range of self-help projects is limited by the difficulty of accumulating capital and by problems in achieving economic self-sufficiency for a small group within a highly technical and interdependent society. Only a few poor people's organizations have been able to create new job opportunities for their members without relying on major corporations or federal funds. Other problem areas, such as medical and health needs, require funds far beyond what most poor people's organizations have or can get.

Still, there is a great deal to be said for using self-help techniques, even in situations where the power structure is in a position to deal with the problems. Any concession the power structure makes to poor people—unless forced from it by poor people themselves—carries with it the price.of increased dependence. This in turn reinforces the power structure and the system itself at a time when the goal of poor people should be to undermine the power structure and change the system. Through self-help, poor people can build and reinforce their own separate power base, rather than that of the power structure.

Cooperatives have in practice been the most effective organizational form for self-help programs. Cooperatives are basically corporations structured along one-person, one-vote lines, whose main goal is the improved welfare of their members. Their incorporated status allows them flexibility in providing goods and services to their members and at the same time protects their members' individual interests. Their structure encourages democratic decision making, membership participation, and leadership development. Cooperatives, by emphasizing the rights and dignity of each individual member, provide an alternative to the use of traditional organizational structures, in which an individual's position depends on his or her power and ability to exercise it in any way necessary.

In practice, cooperatives have been able to deal creatively and effectively with a number of problems. Some of the programs that have been effective include—

- ◆ cooperatively run factories and industrial plants, in which workers control the business and distribution of profits
- ◆ distribution systems for goods produced by members, such as crafts and agricultural products
- ◆ consumer systems that sell quality goods, including food, clothing, drugs, petroleum products, automotive parts, and farm equipment, to members; distribute profits to members in proportion to their purchases; and use profits to develop other programs
- ◆ transportation systems providing good service at low cost
- ◆ nonprofit day care facilities, especially for children of working parents
- ◆ construction of housing units for rent or sale to members

◆ construction, maintenance, and operation of electrical, water, phone, sewage, and garbage collection systems

◆ operation of nursing and old-age homes

◆ cooperative insurance plans to provide low-cost medical, life, and burial insurance

◆ medical, dental, and legal clinics, in which employees are hired directly by the cooperative

◆ construction of recreational facilities

◆ purchase of land to develop housing, industrial sites, small business sites, and recreational facilities

◆ cooperative fire departments to provide protection in areas where it isn't otherwise available

◆ educational programs to provide members with needed education and training

◆ credit unions to provide loans at reasonable cost, especially to those who would otherwise be unable to get credit.

The organizer and members of the poor people's organization should use the same procedures in planning for self-help projects as for other strategic situations. Problems should be analyzed both in terms of their objective characteristics and of how people in the community react to them emotionally. Resources, both human and financial, should be evaluated. A general strategy for carrying out the project should be planned that takes into account the goals of the project itself and the development of membership participation and leadership in the organization. It is important to recognize that as the organization begins to take on economic functions, such as purchasing, distributing, selling stock, paying dividends, giving credit, and allocating capital resources, the opportunity for conflict among members is increased. The tendency some members have to use the organization for personal financial ends must be offset by increased membership education and by developing opportunities for members to participate in planning and decision making.

The problems involved in running a credit union, for example, are in some ways typical of what may happen in a poor people's business operation. A credit union is basically a cooperative savings and loan operation. Members invest their savings in the credit union and in turn are allowed to borrow from it at low interest rates. Because most poor people have immediate credit needs, most members will want to borrow from the credit union as soon as they join. But because poor people have little money to save, the credit union will accumulate cash very slowly. The credit union's directors will have to decide which members will get the first loans, and often those members who are turned down or deferred will be resentful. This can cause a split between the leadership of the credit union and some of the membership. Again, when members fail to repay loans or are late in paying them back, the directors must decide on what action to take. This can easily destroy much of the unity and mutual trust within the credit union, especially if repossessions are made or other legal action is taken.

One of the hardest problems any organization faces in developing self-help projects is getting money. Although some self-help projects can be carried out at low cost, there are a number of others—housing, business development, land acquisition, industrial development, transportation systems, utility systems, medical clinics, community facilities—that require considerable amounts of money. In most rural areas, it is impossible for poor people's organizations to borrow large amounts from conventional local lending sources. The three alternatives that have proved most effective for poor people's organizations faced with the problem of capital accumulation have been to raise the money through their membership; to seek outside private help from individuals, foundations, and religious institutions; and to seek federal funds.

Much local fundraising is done informally. Chicken suppers, barbecues, fish fries, bingo games, raffles, dances, and parties can be used to raise considerable sums—although in some areas many of these activities may be considered improper by some people. Usually, though, a poor people's organization must also have more regular ways of bringing in money. One way is by selling shares of stock to members and nonmembers. The price of a share should be low enough that poor people can afford to purchase it. Stock designed for sale to poor people should be issued in denominations of $10, $5, or even $100. Provisions should be made for purchase of a share in weekly or monthly payments, so that even the poorest members have a chance to participate. Sometimes purchase of one share of stock is made a requirement for membership in the organization. In a poor people's organization that is structured as a cooperative, however, each member must be limited to one vote, no matter how many shares of stock she or he owns. If stock is to be sold to persons other than the poor, and in cases when purchase of a share entitles the purchaser to membership in the organization, nonvoting stock should also be issued. This will prevent outside interests from gaining a voice in the conduct of the poor people's business.

These nonvoting shares can be sold in a number of ways. Personal contacts with rich liberals, foundations, and religious leaders can be very effective. Mailing lists are available with the names of liberal donors, magazine subscribers, and agency members. For a small cost a brochure can be sent to several hundred persons. A sample brochure might read in part:

> Some of you may have been reading with interest of the recent decision by the Ford Foundation to put a proportion of its investment capital into what the foundation termed "high social yield" issues. Such stocks, issued by poor people's cooperatives and corporations, are not "glamour" or "blue chip" issues, but they offer something more important: the opportunity for poor people to develop constructive and positive alternatives to the repression and violence of our society.

> The members of the Brown County Progress Association, Inc., a group of 75 poor farmers who were evicted from their homes after attempting to register to vote, have raised by their own efforts $4,500 to purchase land on which to rebuild their homes and farms. An option has been purchased on 300 acres—but $6,500 is needed to make the necessary down payment before the option expires. To meet this crisis, the association has issued 650 shares of nonvoting stock at $10 par value per share. These shares are now available to those who support the goals and principles of the association.

For those who have been a part of the struggle for human rights, now is the time to broaden your stock portfolio—with an investment in human dignity.

One note of caution—if sales of stock are solicited across state lines, the transaction may come under the regulations of the Securities and Exchange Commission. A number of potential investors may also be concerned with the relation of such an investment to their tax deductions. It may be worthwhile to point out that, should the investment not be recovered, it can be deducted as a capital loss.

A number of persons may be interested in making direct, tax-exempt contributions to the poor people's organization. Because most poor people's organizations do not have tax-exempt status, the organizer should arrange for the money to be donated to an organization that is tax-exempt, earmarked for a grant to the poor people's organization.

Foundations are a traditional source of funds for poor people's organizations. Most of the grants to organizations that are run by and for poor people have been made by a handful of foundations. The liberal foundations tend to see their role as innovative and experimental and are more interested in making new projects possible than in financing ongoing programs. Proposals written for these foundations should stress the pilot aspects of the proposed projects and the possibilities they offer as new alternatives applicable to other areas and situations. There is little point in trying to "hustle" these foundations; their personnel are usually extremely knowledgeable about what makes for effective poor people's organizations. Before preparing a foundation proposal, it is helpful to send for a copy of the annual report—sometimes available at libraries—for each foundation the proposal will be sent to. From these reports, which list and often describe all programs that received grants that year, a sense of the foundation's goals and priorities can be gained. A number of religious groups are also showing increasing interest in community organizing projects and can be approached for funds.

Countless federal programs for "individual and community improvement" exist on paper. Realistically, however, few of these resources are available to poor people's organizations. Most federal funds supposedly destined for the poor actually wind up in the hands of public and private agencies, universities, and corporations. Various federal agencies publish catalogs listing the different programs available.

It should not be assumed that because a poor people's organization emphasizes self-help programs rather than power tactics or political organizing, it will not be opposed by the power structure. On the contrary, many power structures feel most threatened by the possibility of independent economic progress by poor people. The probable reactions of the power structure should be carefully considered in developing the strategy for initiating a self-help project. For example, in one area a poor people's organization opened a cooperative grocery store to provide quality food at fair prices to its members. As poor people began to shift their business to the co-op and away from the local "credit stores," the credit store operators began to demand immediate payment in full of debts owed them. Those poor people who could not pay were threatened with sentences at the state penitentiary. Only by locating funds to loan to these persons to pay off their accounts was the organization able to relieve the pressure and maintain its volume of business. Such measures have proved to be common whenever poor people's organizations entered into economic competition with local interests. The organization that emphasizes self-help, as much as the one that emphasizes power tactics or politics, can expect any of the reprisals against its members of which the power structure is capable.

If successful, however, such projects can be of great value as part of the struggle of poor people for equality. By providing an independent economic base, they decrease the dependence of poor people on the power structure, thus weakening the power structure's hold on the community and paving the way for successful political or power campaigns. By providing needed goods and services at reduced costs and by providing opportunities to work and produce at decent wages, they improve living conditions for the poor in the community. Finally, by involving members in such processes as education, decision making, and leadership, they help build the self-confidence, self-reliance, and self-esteem of the members and the strength of the poor people's organization itself.

 Chapter 11

Leaving the Community

One of the things the organizer must always keep in mind is that one day she may leave the community she is working in. The time of departure can be very difficult for both the organizer and the community. The organizer who works in a community for several years becomes deeply involved in it and deeply attached to it. Very real and sincere friendships develop between the organizer and the people she works with. Most organizers, no matter how much they guard against it, do come to identify in some degree with the poor people in the community, their goals, and their organizations. The organizer also knows that she is leaving this to move on to a new area, a new situation, with new problems, difficulties, and dangers, and that having completed one job, she now has the responsibility to start another one from nothing.

Nevertheless, it is essential that the organizer recognize when the right time has come for her to leave the community and that she leave at that time. There are people who have come into communities as organizers and stayed on as community leaders, which is all right if the person intends to spend the rest of her life in a community. But most organizers come into a community to develop leaders, not to be leaders. By staying in the community past the time for her to leave, the organizer inhibits the development of community leadership and independence. It is important for poor people in a community to become free not only of their dependence on the power structure but also of their dependence on the organizer. It can be as harmful to a community for an organizer to stay after she has completed her job as for her to leave before she has finished it.

The time the organizer must spend in a community may vary from several months to many years. What is important, though, is not the time spent, but what has happened in that time. The organizer must analyze what has been accomplished in the community since she arrived. She should evaluate the attitudes of poor people in the community, the skills and abilities of leaders, the structure and functioning of the poor people's organization or organizations, the state of ongoing projects, the nature of remaining needs, the concrete accomplishments to date, the political strength of the poor, and the relation of the power structure to the poor community. The organizer should ask the following questions, organized by general areas of concern, as part of her evaluation of community change.

Attitudes of the Poor

- ◆ To what extent do poor people in the community have a good understanding of community problems and their causes?
- ◆ How openly do poor people now express their concern with these problems and their elimination?
- ◆ How willing are poor people to take action to deal with these problems, even when it involves significant risk to themselves and their families?
- ◆ To what extent do poor people identify with the goals and programs of the poor people's organization?
- ◆ How well do poor people identify with leaders from their own community or from their racial, gender, or class group?

Leadership

- ◆ Has the "established" leadership of the poor community been replaced with new and dynamic leaders of the poor drawn from within the poor community itself?

- Are these leaders truly representative of the poor community's needs and desires?
- Do these leaders reliably represent the ideas of the poor community, even under pressure?
- Do these leaders actively encourage broad participation in decision making, even at the cost of their own personal power?
- How well have these leaders learned the skills of the organizer in such areas as problem analysis, resource analysis, strategy development, tactical planning, communications, education, and training?
- How capable would these leaders be of serving as organizers themselves in other communities?

Poor People's Organizations

- Has an active and effective poor people's organization been developed in the community?
- Do a large number of the poor people participate actively in the organization?
- How well do the members understand the nature, structure, purposes, and programs of the organization?
- How responsive is the leadership of the organization to the needs and desires of its members?
- How successful has the organization been in eliminating community problems?
- How well has the organization planned its strategy for the future?

Projects

- What types of projects is the poor people's organization running?
- How many basic needs of poor people in the community are being met by these programs?
- How effectively are the projects meeting these needs?
- How many of the organization's members are involved in these projects as participants, planners, and decision makers?

◆ How effective are those projects in motivating poor people toward further participation and action?

◆ How well do these projects help give poor people a sense of their own individual and group identity and dignity?

Accomplishments

◆ How many problems of the poor community has the poor people's organization tried to deal with?

◆ How well have different types of tactics been used?

◆ What significant changes for the better have been made in these problems?

◆ What major defeats has the organization had?

◆ What improvements have been made in the lives of individual poor people in the community?

Political Strength

◆ How many of the poor people have registered to vote?

◆ How many of these people voted in the last election?

◆ How many poor people ran as candidates in the last election?

◆ How many of these were elected? How responsive have they been to the needs of the poor community? How successful have they been in meeting these needs?

◆ How effectively has the poor community exercised its voting strength in elections between nonpoor candidates?

◆ What concessions were demanded as the price of this support? How many of these were carried out after the election?

Power Structure Relations

◆ Has the power structure become more responsive to the needs of the poor?

◆ What concrete changes have been made by the power structure to help the poor community?

- What changes have been made in the operation of public agencies to make them more responsive to the needs of the poor?
- To what extent does the power structure recognize the poor people's organization as representing and speaking for the poor people of the community?
- To what extent are the real leaders of the poor community recognized as such by the power structure?
- How many poor people now occupy positions of leverage in the power structure?

This analysis is not only one that the organizer makes just before he leaves, though; it is an analysis he is continually making during his work in the community. In a sense these points help define the goals toward which he works.

There is one more question that must be answered before the organizer leaves the community: How dependent are the poor people on him? If the organizer has done his job right, the poor people should be free of dependence on him by the time he leaves. To achieve this, the organizer must be willing to keep a back seat at all times, to deliberately submerge himself, and to accept the resentment that many members of the poor community will feel toward him as he gradually withdraws. Too many organizers find themselves unable to assume this role. Rather than let poor people speak for themselves, they become spokespeople for the poor. They move into leadership positions, instead of helping poor people become leaders themselves. Instead of teaching poor people all their skills, they keep their organizing techniques to themselves, so that the poor remain dependent on them. Instead of remaining in the background, they become the center of action and attention: negotiating with the power structure when poor people should be speaking, writing proposals that the poor should develop, making decisions when poor people should decide. Far from helping the poor community to achieve self-sufficiency, such organizers consciously or unconsciously manipulate it for their own ends.

Avoiding the above problems, however, will not necessarily make the process of leaving the community any easier. As soon as the organizer feels that the time to leave is approaching, he should begin to prepare the community for that day. He should begin to be absent from planning sessions, strategy meetings, and community gatherings—at first occasionally, later frequently. Only through the experience of working without the organizer can community people begin to believe in their own ability to continue the work of organizing without him. In the last analysis, the only people who will help poor people are poor people, and it is important that the organizer help people in the community to realize this before he leaves.

The organizer should take the same careful, deliberate approach to leaving the community he took to entering it. He should let his key contacts know as soon as possible that he will be leaving so that they can be involved in planning for his departure. The organizer can honestly present the reasons for his departure, based on the analysis he has made of the community's progress: the changes in the community, the increased political strength of poor people, the programs in operation, the skills of the leadership and the community as a whole, the successes achieved by the poor people's organization. Poor people in the community will often not have the same perspective as the organizer. Being directly involved, they may not realize the importance of what they have done. The victories, even more than the defeats, will have been forgotten. By emphasizing their accomplishments, the organizer will be expressing his confidence in their ability to carry on without him.

During her final weeks in the community, the organizer should make an effort to see as many of the people she knows as possible. She should visit the different poor people she has worked with and attend meetings of block clubs, committees, and organizations in the community. Under no circumstances should she simply disappear, however strong the temptation to avoid the personally difficult work of saying goodbye.

It is usually a good idea to pay a visit to those members of the power structure the organizer has had contact with. In these visits, the organizer should suggest that her absence from the community will probably be temporary and that she will come back if the poor people need her. Such a suggestion will often temper any plans the power structure might have for cracking down on poor people once the organizer leaves.

It is not suggested that the organizer break all contact with the community once she has actually left it. Especially during the first few months, it is helpful to pay occasional visits to the community. If this is not possible, the organizer should maintain contact with key members of the poor community by phone. This continued contact will help offset any sense of abandonment or lack of direction some members of the poor community may feel. The organizer should also be sure that someone in the poor community knows where she can be contacted at all times, in case they feel they need her advice, in particular on technical details of strategy, tactics, and resources. The organizer should leave the community in such a way that she can always come back if necessary. The knowledge that she is still available to help the community if it needs her will help give poor people the confidence to work so effectively that the organizer will never need to return.

I Have Seen Freedom

My hands are as cracked as an August field
That's burned in the sun for a hundred years
With furrows so deep you could hide yourself
But I ain't planting cotton no more this year
I'll just sit on the porch with my eagle eye
And watch for a change of wind
The rows are as straight as a shotgun barrel
And long as a bullet can spin

You know how hot it gets in Mississippi
You know how dry it gets in the summer sun
The dust clouds swirl all down the Delta
I just hope that I don't die 'fore the harvest comes

Black clouds gathering on the edge of town
But no rain's gonna fall on us
Hoes rise and fall in a distant field
Earth takes a beating for all of us
I thought I heard the angel of death overhead
But it's only the cropduster's plane
Hoes rise and fall like the beating of wings
Lord send us freedom and rain

You know how hot it gets in Mississippi
You know how dry it gets in the summer sun
The dust clouds swirl all down the Delta
I just hope that I don't die 'fore the harvest comes

There was neither rain
nor freedom
in Forrest City, Arkansas
the place where I spent
the summer of 1965

It was a stopping place
first on the railway
then on the road
that runs from Memphis to Little Rock

A farming town
set down in the furrows and dust
of the Mississippi River Delta
in the heart of what was in those days called
the "Black Belt"
that crescent of black land and black people
stretching from Virginia to East Texas
that once marked the boundaries
of cotton
and of slavery

The town had in fact been founded
by the Confederate cavalry leader
General Nathan Bedford Forrest
and in the summer of 1965
that town was doing its best
to live up to its name
and to its namesake

I have not been back to Forrest City
since I left almost 30 years ago
so I don't know what has changed since then
But in that summer of 1965
it was a typical Southern county seat:
a red brick courthouse in the center
fields of cotton and soybeans
radiating out from the town
in rows as long as the eye cared to look
in the violent sun
of an Arkansas summer

There was the usual assortment
of small-town, farm-town businesses:
cotton gin, feed store
truck lot, tractor dealer
even, in a gesture to changing Southern times
a factory that made fork lifts

And the usual assortment of small-town officials:
a police chief named Gunn
a city attorney named Sharp
even an FBI agent named Smart
and then two of almost everything else:
a black high school
and a white high school;
white restaurants
where blacks couldn't go
and black restaurants
where whites wouldn't go;
black barber shops, bars and beauty parlors;
white barber shops, bars and beauty parlors;
a white funeral home
and a black funeral home

a river of hatred and fear
ran down the social center of town
violently dividing black and white
as certainly as the Mississippi River
forty miles to the east
divided the state of Arkansas
from the states of Mississippi and Tennessee

But in that summer of 1965
Forrest City had something else
something new
which was beginning to wear away
at the stone walls
of ignorance and fear
of segregation and discrimination
of racism and violence
that had been built up
along with the town

Forrest City
had a freedom movement
a field office
of the Student Nonviolent Coordinating Committee
comfortably and commonly known by its initials as SNCC
the militant student wing
of the Southern freedom movement

SNCC and that freedom movement
were centered and headquartered
in the black funeral home
where Ms. Florence Clay
ministered to the living and to the dead
and where we SNCC volunteers
slept fitfully at best

all too aware of the living dangers
in the night outside
cruising by in cop cars and pickup trucks
and of the dead
lying in their satin-lined caskets
in the chapel downstairs

I had grown up
in a Pennsylvania mountain town
not much bigger than Forrest City
and had gone to a consolidated high school
where I'd learned carpentry
along with a teenage taste for auto mechanics

and so I had been recruited
by the northern friends of SNCC
and of the black freedom movement
to help build freedom centers
in places like Forrest City

So there behind the new funeral home
built of brick and block
in the old wood frame building
which had been abandoned for years
we put up siding and sheet rock
rolled out roofing and Romex cable
ran water and sewer lines
built school tables and library shelves
so that the black children of Forrest City
could come to the freedom center
to study and learn the history which had been denied them
their own history
so that they could learn what freedom was all about

Outside the freedom center
in the unpaved streets and shotgun shacks
in the beauty parlors and barber shops
in the churches and restaurants
in the bars and pool halls
where the black community of Forrest City
lived and breathed

There in the stubborn heat
of an Arkansas summer
something else was being pieced and pulled
planned and measured
hammered and honed
built and born:
a black movement for freedom

And though the white folks talked
of "outside agitators"
of "communists" and "race mixers"
this movement for freedom
was bred and born in the bone
imagined, shaped and formed
lived, loved and led
by local folk
by people like Ms. Florence Clay at the funeral home
keeping watch from her upstairs window
as the pickup trucks and police cars
sped by in the night

By people like Mervin Barr
born and raised in Forrest City
where there was not much of a future
for a bright young man
whose skin was black

So Mervin Barr
seeking a better future for himself
had enlisted in the United States Marines
and was sent to boot camp at Parris Island
where, because he was black and outspoken
he was beaten so badly
that his kidneys never worked right again

Mervin Barr would die
before the year 1965 ended
refusing to go for treatment
yet another time
to the Veterans Hospital in Memphis
because that would have meant
not marching through the streets of Forrest City
with his neighbors and friends
after he had asked them, begged them
pleaded, cajoled, preached, agitated, talked
walking the streets day after day, night after night
in the heat and dust of an Arkansas summer
raising his voice
talking his heart out
giving his life for freedom

> Have you heard of General Nathan Bedford Forrest
> For five years he fought the Yankees hand to hand
> But after Appomatox he got lonesome
> So he went and organized the Ku Klux Klan
> His ex-soldiers crossed the Mississippi River
> And they founded Forrest City, Arkansas
> I never got to meet old General Forrest
> But then he never met my old friend Mervin Barr

> All along the bars and grills of Forrest City
> Talking to the people where they are

"I think it's time for us to get together
There's no need to be afraid" says Mervin Barr
Shooting pool to supplement the pension
From injuries he got in the Marines
When he talked you couldn't help but listen
He was the gentlest man I've ever seen

Some days he was too sick to leave the south side
Where he lived with his momma in a little old shotgun shack
So they'd send him to the V.A. home in Memphis
Where the sheets were white but Mervin's face was black
But he knew that he was needed by his people
And he marched them up and down that Delta town
The doctors tried to send him back to Memphis
But he wouldn't leave until the fight was won

They say that on the day that he was buried
Five hundred people stood beside his grave
I don't like funerals, but I kind of wish I'd been there
Though I couldn't say just why I feel that way
The nightriders' shotguns didn't kill him
Nor the people that had sworn they'd do him in
He died because he wouldn't go to Memphis
And I don't expect to see his like again

But while in one sense it is true
that I have never again seen the like
of this person, this time, this place

It is also true
that what I learned in the summer of 1965
I learn again and again
in my daily work
as an organizer
in the Southern United States

for what is now almost thirty years
surprisingly still here
hopefully still working and fighting
for freedom

the memories, the images, the stories
of that time and place
are my guideposts, my highway signs
on this long and winding road
I keep trying to walk
together with you

I remember Reverend Sherman Jones
preaching at the Salem Baptist Church
on the west side of Forrest City
and telling us:

"Whenever you have a birth
you have three things that go with it:
blood, pain and water.

Some folks want the birth
but they don't want the blood
or the pain or the tears;

but if you want the one
you've got to take the other with it."

I remember this story
and I remind myself, I tell myself:
There are no easy answers
no promises, no guarantees
sometimes not even a good long shot
but because the road is hard and long

and because as blues singer Robert Johnson said
there are "stones in our pathway"
we have no choice
except to get started right now

And this reminds me of a story
from my own Jewish tradition:

A very old man is sitting with a friend
in front of his house.
And he tells the friend:
"Tomorrow I'm going to plant a fig tree."

His friend looks at him and says,
"You're crazy.
A fig tree doesn't bear fruit for generations.
You'll die years before that ever happens.
Maybe your grandchildren will eat the fruit—
but not you."

The old man turns, looks at his friend and says:
"In that case,
I'd better plant the tree today."

And I remind myself, I tell myself
in another saying from Jewish tradition:
"It is not your responsibility
to finish the job;
but you are also not free
from the obligation to begin
and to do your part."

And because after so many years
memories run together
like smaller rivers feeding the Mississippi

I also remember the story told by a poor white preacher
from the Appalachian mountains
Clinton Patrick of Cob Hill, Kentucky:
"They say one night Roosevelt couldn't sleep.
Well, his wife asked him what was the matter
and he said:

'I keep hearing the hungry children crying.
You know, I ordered them to plow under all that wheat
and I can't sleep
for hearing the children crying for bread.'
She said, 'Well, why don't you put cotton in your ears?'
He said, 'I can't.
I had that plowed under too.' "

And I remind myself, I tell myself:
People without power
can only rely on themselves
and not on those who have power
however well-intentioned

I remember sitting in the Salem Baptist Church
the church where Reverend Sherman Jones told the story
of birth, blood, pain and tears
listening to the Freedom Singers
(one of whom was Bernice Johnson Reagon
founder of Sweet Honey in the Rock
who is still singing for freedom after all these years)

I remember sitting listening and singing
as those voices joined in powerful unity lifted us
not just out of our seats
but out of ourselves
out of our everyday lives
out of our insecurities, out of our fears

and into a dream, into the imagination
of the harmony of freedom

And I remind myself, I tell myself:
Power alone is not enough
Even as we struggle to change
who owns, who rules, who decides
we must also open up the human heart
to the freedom to love
whomever one chooses
to the freedom to live
however one needs to live
to the freedom to laugh
in the voice that is uniquely our own
no matter who is listening

I sometimes remember, too
how hopeless it all sometimes seemed
how impossible, how foolish
to dream of freedom
having been enslaved so long

And I tell myself, I remind myself:
Be careful
as you organize with people
not to sell them short
with "strategies" and "tactics"
based on "what is winnable"
and "what is possible"

but rather let yourself be guided
by *their* vision
of what is right
of what is just
of what is true

however far off or impossible
that vision may seem
because freedom
always has been
and always will be
a far off and impossible dream

And finally
I tell myself, I remind myself:
On the one hand, it's simply not true
that because of the black freedom movement
everything changed overnight

Drive down any Southern highway today
turn to the right or to the left
anywhere the gravel meets the blacktop
turn again when the gravel changes
to dirt or sand or mud
and it is still the summer of 1965
the sagging porches, the broken lives
the bitter shacks, the barren yards
old cars and dreams stripped bare
the violent legacy of racism, segregation, and slavery

Down too many Southern roads
time has stood as still
as the air on an Arkansas summer night
in the cotton and soybean fields
along the Mississippi River

But on the other hand
it's also not true
that nothing has changed

because freedom
as the old hymn and freedom song tells us
truly is "a constant struggle"
a daily act
a way of everyday life

Freedom is a "habit of resistance"
an acquired taste for saying "no" to injustice
a conditioned reflex
for helping others
stand up and speak out

Freedom is not
the safe harbor
at the end of the journey

Freedom is the journey itself
every day of our lives
every step of the way

> *When our lives that follow fields of cotton*
> *Burn and crack like sun-baked clay*
> *We will gather at the deepest river*
> *Longing for a new day*

>> *Though the night divides us from each other*
>> *Though the days are hard and long*
>> *When we walk along this road together*
>> *We are strong*
>> *We are strong*

> *When the years of dust have choked our voices*
> *'Til there's not a word to say*
> *We will look to where the plow is turning*
> *Longing for a new day*

Though the night divides us from each other
Though the days are hard and long
When we walk along this road together
We are strong
We are strong

When we look to each other for courage
Strong when we tear down the stone walls between us

In the silence of a world gone crazy
Truth and justice lose their way
We are gathered at the edge of midnight
Longing for a new day

Though the night divides us from each other
Though the days are hard and long
When we walk along this road together
We are strong
We are strong

In the end
what I learned almost 30 years ago
in the dust and heat of an Arkansas summer
has become the core of values and beliefs
that shapes my everyday life and work:

I believe that ordinary people
are in fact often quite extraordinary
capable of remarkable wisdom
unusual stubbornness
and great courage

but I also believe
that often these same ordinary people carry within them
the capacity for outrageous violence
for doing great damage and harm to others

for undoing what love and care
what courage and wisdom have built

and that whether any of our lives
are lived for good or for evil
depends at least in part
on whether we have a vision of a better world
in which to trust and to believe
and a chance to act in ways
that bring that vision
that better world
a step or two closer
to where we stand today

I believe that the most profound leadership
as well as the most effective
is that which flows
from the grassroots up
rather than down from the top

I believe that a person's capacity for leadership
is often in inverse proportion
to the discrimination and exclusion
they have personally experienced—
which explains why, in our time
so much visionary and transforming leadership
has come from African Americans
and other people of color
from women of different colors and classes
from poor and working people of different races

I believe that in the end
those who are now excluded and exploited

will get what they deserve
only through their own action
by organizing together
by building collective power
and by demanding change

Because freedom
can not be given
but must be taken

Equity and parity
can not be negotiated
but must be appropriated

Respect
can not be requested
but must be demanded

Dignity and self-esteem
can not be bestowed
but must be earned

Finally, I believe
that it is in the very process and act
of working and fighting for freedom
that a person
or a people
becomes free

It is not
when we arrive at our destination
but when we take the first step
on our journey
that liberation begins

It is when we join with others
in an irrevocable decision
that all people must be free
that we ourselves
can see freedom

> *I read in the paper, I watched on the show*
> *They said that it happened a long time ago*
> *The years had gone by, I just didn't know*
> > *Working for freedom now*
> *The songs that we sang still ring in my ears*
> *The hope and the glory, the pain and the fears*
> *I just can't believe it's been twenty-five years*
> > *Working for freedom now*

> > *Been a long time, but I keep on trying*
> > *For I know where I am bound*
> > *Been a hard road, but I don't mind dying*
> > *I have seen freedom*

> *Sometimes we stumble, sometimes we fall*
> *Sometimes we stand with our backs to the wall*
> *This road will humble the proudest of all*
> > *Working for freedom now*
> *Though the road up ahead may stretch out far and long*
> *We must always remember the roads that we've gone*
> *Memory will help us to keep keeping on*
> > *Working for freedom now*

> > *Been a long time, but I keep on trying*
> > *For I know where I am bound*
> > *Been a hard road, but I don't mind dying*
> > *I have seen freedom*

Those who have fallen and given their last
Have passed on to us what remains of their task
To fight for the future and pray for the past
Working for freedom now
The song of their laughter, the step of their feet
The voice of their pain that cries out in our sleep
Will be judged in the end by the faith that we keep
Working for freedom now

Been a long time, but I keep on trying
For I know where I am bound
Been a hard road, but I don't mind dying
I have seen freedom

The wind in the winter is bitter and chill
The cries of the hunted are heard on the hill
I just can't believe there's such suffering still
Working for freedom now
The wind blows the summer from fields far away
We stand in the dust in the heat of the day
Our hearts stopped so still that there's nothing to say
Working for freedom now

Been a long time, but I keep on trying
For I know where I am bound
Been a hard road, but I don't mind dying
I have seen freedom

September 20, 1993

The Goals of Organizing

Somewhere in the Deep South, on the road that runs from New Orleans to Atlanta, an 80-year-old woman is living alone in a shack by the roadside. If you are driving along that road, you can sometimes see her going painfully along in the long grass beside the highway. She is looking for the drink bottles the motorists throw out the windows of their cars as they go past at 70 miles an hour. Tomorrow a child will come by her shack to collect the bottles and bring them to the grocery downtown and will bring the 5 cents a bottle she gets back to the old woman to buy food.

Or if you were walking the dirt streets of a town not far from there some six months ago, you might have seen a child playing in the road. He is throwing his toy into the air, chasing it, picking it up, throwing it and chasing again. You come closer. It is a dead bird.

Make no mistake. Organizing is not just about strategies, about analyses, about tactics. Organizing is about people, about the old woman with her drink bottles and the child with his dead bird. Organizing is about the "welfare cheats," the "deadbeats," the "punks"—everyone else this society locks out and shuts in.

If anyone else still has illusions about this country, it's not poor people. They know that this country will spend $20 billion to put someone on the moon but will not spend $20 to put someone on their feet. They know it will spend more to keep boll weevils from eating the cotton than to keep rats from eating the fingers of a baby in Harlem or Appalachia. They know it has paid a U.S. senator over $100,000 a year not to plant cotton, but would not pay $1 to the families on his plantation not to raise hookworms in the stomachs of their own children.

What would she or he say, that famous poor person the "leaders" of this country so often talk about, and so rarely talk with, if given the chance to speak?

That I needed a home, and you gave me food stamps;
That I needed a job, and you got me on the welfare;
That my family was sick, and you gave us your used clothes;
That I needed my pride and dignity as a human being, and you gave me surplus beans.

Let us not forget, when we talk of violence, that the death of a young mother in childbirth is violent, that the slow starvation of the mind and body of a child is violent. Let us not forget that hunger is violent, that pain is violent, that oppression is violent, that early death is violent. And that the death of hope is the most violent of all.

The organizer brings hope to the people.

Suggested Reading

Adams, F. (1975). *Unearthing seeds of fire: The idea of Highlander*. Winston-Salem, NC: John F. Blair.

Alinsky, S. D. (1946). *Reveille for radicals*. New York: Vintage Books.

Alinsky, S. D. (1969). *Rules for radicals: A pragmatic primer for realistic radicals*. New York: Vintage Books.

Bloom, J. (1987). *Class, race, and the civil rights movement*. Bloomington: Indiana University Press.

Bobo, K., Kendall, J., & Max, S. (1991). *Organizing for social change: A manual for activists in the 1990s*. Cabin John, MD: Seven Locks Press.

Boyte, H. C. (1984). *Community is possible: Repairing America's roots*. New York: Harper & Row.

Boyte, H. C. (1989). *Commonwealth: A return to citizen politics*. New York: Free Press.

Brager, G., & Specht, H. (1973). *Community organizing*. New York: Columbia University Press.

Brecher, J. (1972). *Strike!* San Francisco: Straight Arrow Books.

Breines, W. (1989). *Community organization in the New Left 1962–1968: The great refusal*. New Brunswick, NJ: Rutgers University Press.

Bulkin, E., Pratt, M. B., & Smith, B. (1984). *Yours in struggle: Three feminist perspectives on anti-semitism and racism*. Ithaca, NY: Firebrand Books.

Burghardt, S. (1982). *Organizing for community action*. Beverly Hills, CA: Sage.

Burghardt, S. (1982). *The other side of organizing.* Cambridge, MA: Schenkman Publishing.

Carson, C. (1981). *In struggle: SNCC and the black awakening of the 1960s.* Cambridge, MA: Harvard University Press.

Chafe, W. H. (1980). *Civilities and civil rights.* New York: Oxford University Press.

Cloward, R., & Piven, F. F. (1975). *The politics of turmoil.* New York: Vintage Books.

Cluster, D. (Ed.). (1979). *They should have served that cup of coffee: Seven radicals remember the 60s.* Boston: South End Press.

Davis, A. (1983). *Women, race and class.* New York: Vintage Books.

Delgado, G. (1986). *Organizing the movement: The roots and growth of ACORN.* Philadelphia: Temple University Press.

Du Bois, W. E. B. (1964). *Black reconstruction in America, 1860–1880.* Cleveland: Meridian.

Ecklein, J. (1984). *Community organizing.* New York: Free Press.

Evans, S. M. (1979). *Personal politics: The roots of women's liberation in the civil rights movement and the New Left.* New York: Alfred A. Knopf.

Evans, S. M. (1989). *Born for liberty: A history of women in America.* New York: Free Press.

Evans, S. M., & Boyte, H. C. (1986). *Free spaces: The sources of democratic change in America.* New York: Harper & Row.

Fanon, F. (1967). *Black skin, white masks.* New York: Grove Press.

Fanon, F. (1968). *The wretched of the earth.* New York: Evergreen.

Fink, D. (1983). *The radical vision of Saul Alinsky.* Maryknoll, NY: Orbis Books.

Flacks, R. (1990). *Making history: The American Left and the American mind.* New York: Columbia University Press.

Flanagan, J. (1981). *The successful volunteer organization.* Chicago: Contemporary Books.

Flanagan, J. (1982). *The grass roots fundraising book.* Chicago: Contemporary Books.

Flexner, E. (1971). *Century of struggle.* New York: Atheneum.

Giddings, P. (1984). *When and where I enter: The impact of black women on race and sex in America.* New York: William Morrow.

Harding, V. (1980). *The other American revolution.* Los Angeles: University of California, Center for Afro-American Studies.

Harding, V. (1981). *There is a river: The black struggle for freedom in America*. New York: Harcourt Brace Jovanovich.

Horton, M., Kohl, J., & Kohl, H. (1990). *The long haul: An autobiography*. New York: Doubleday.

Kahn, S. (1991). *Organizing: A guide for grassroots leaders*. Silver Spring, MD: NASW Press.

Kaufman, J. (1988). *Broken alliance: The turbulent times between blacks and Jews in America*. New York: Charles Scribner's Sons.

King, M. L., Jr. (1958). *Stride toward freedom*. New York: Harper & Row.

King, M. L., Jr. (1963). *Why we can't wait*. New York: New American Library.

King, M. L., Jr. (1967). *Where do we go from here: Chaos or community?* New York: Beacon Press.

Lerner, G. (1972). *Black women in white America*. New York: Pantheon Books.

Lerner, G. (1979). *The majority finds its past: Placing women in history*. New York: Oxford University Press.

Malcolm X. (1987). *Autobiography of Malcolm X*. New York: Ballantine Books.

Memmi, A. (1967). *The colonizer and the colonized*. Boston: Beacon Press.

Minnich, E. K. (1990). *Transforming knowledge*. Philadelphia: Temple University Press.

Moody, A. (1968). *Coming of age in Mississippi*. New York: Dell.

Moraga, C., & Anzaldua, G. (1981). *This bridge called my back*. Watertown, MA: Persephone Press.

Morris, A. (1984). *Origins of the civil rights movement*. New York: Free Press/Macmillan.

Mother Jones. (1976). *The autobiography of Mother Jones*. Chicago: Charles H. Kerr.

Pharr, S. (1988). *Homophobia: A weapon of sexism*. Inverness, CA: Chardon Press.

Piven, F. F., & Cloward, R. A. (1978). *Poor people's movements: Why they succeed, how they fail*. New York: Random House.

Raines, H. (1977). *My soul is rested*. New York: G. P. Putnam's Sons.

Rosengarten, T. (1974). *All God's dangers: The life of Nate Shaw*. New York: Alfred A. Knopf.

Shellow, J. R., & Stella, N. C. (1989). *Grant seekers guide.* Mt. Kisco, NY: Moyer Bell.

Staples, L. (1984). *Roots to power: A manual for grassroots organizing.* Westport, CT: Praeger.

Walker, A. (1976). *Meridian.* San Diego: Harcourt Brace Jovanovich.

Williams, J. (1987). *Eyes on the prize.* New York: Penguin Books.

Zinn, H. (1980). *A people's history of the United States.* New York: Harper & Row.

Index

About the Author

Si Kahn has spent more than 25 years working in the southern civil rights, labor, and community organizing movements. He was raised in a small college town in the Pennsylvania mountains, where his father was a rabbi and his mother an artist. His first organizing job was as a volunteer with the Student Nonviolent Coordinating Committee (SNCC) in Forrest City, Arkansas, where he worked registering voters following passage of the Voting Rights Act of 1965.

After several years in Georgia working with African-American farmers' cooperatives and voter registration and electoral campaigns, he moved to the North Georgia mountains and became active in labor work. During the Brookside strike in Harlan County, Kentucky, in 1973–1974, he coordinated the national coalition support effort on behalf of the United Mine Workers of America (UMWA). From 1975 through 1979, he worked with the Amalgamated Clothing & Textile Workers Union (ACTWU) on the J. P. Stevens campaign, first as a consulting strategist to the union and later on the ACTWU staff as an organizer and area director for the campaign. In 1980, he founded Grassroots Leadership to continue the long-term work of building a multiracial movement in the South. He currently serves as Grassroots Leadership's executive director.

A songwriter and folksinger, Kahn has toured with such performers as Cathy Fink and Marcy Marxer, Andy Irvine, John McCutcheon, Jane Sapp, and Pete Seeger. He has recorded nine albums of original songs for adults and children, plus a double album of traditional songs from the civil rights, women's, and labor movements with Jane Sapp and Pete Seeger.

Kahn's two books on the techniques of community organizing (*How People Get Power*, first edition, McGraw-Hill, 1970, and *Organizing: A Guide for Grassroots Leaders*, first edition, McGraw-Hill, 1982; revised edition, NASW Press, 1991) have been used extensively in graduate and undergraduate social work courses. Kahn has given lectures, workshops, and concerts at colleges and universities throughout North America and Europe.

Kahn helped organize and was founding chair of the Jewish Fund for Justice, a national foundation that supports community organizing, and continues to serve on the board. He is currently a doctoral candidate in American Studies specializing in multiracial organizational development at the Union Institute. The father of three children, he is married to the feminist philosopher Elizabeth Kamarch Minnich.

About Grassroots Leadership

Grassroots Leadership, founded by organizer Si Kahn, has provided organizing assistance to social change organizations since 1980. Working from the philosophy that people have the power to solve their own problems creatively, Grassroots Leadership helps organizations achieve the goals they set for themselves.

The multiracial staff share experience and skills in organizational development, plus a deep understanding of the culture and mores of community organizations. They help social change organizations improve their expertise in such areas as multiracial organizing, direct-action campaigns, strategies, tactics, coalitions, fundraising, financial management, and planning, and they provide training in leadership development, meeting skills, public relations, communication, and other areas.

Grassroots Leadership also provides skilled facilitation for meetings and retreats. In addition to folksong concerts, staff and board members offer a speakers bureau with topics on civil rights, organizing, and social change in the 1990s.

For more information on Grassroots Leadership, contact

Grassroots Leadership
1300 Baxter Street, Suite 200
P.O. Box 36006
Charlotte, NC 28236

telephone: 704-332-3090
fax: 704-332-0445

Grassroots Leadership/ NASW Press Tour

In conjunction with the publication of *How People Get Power*, Grassroots Leadership and the NASW Press are sponsoring a lecture and concert tour by Si Kahn and other Grassroots Leadership staff members. They will be available for appearances of one to three days at colleges and universities, as well as state and national conferences. The appearances may include lectures or workshops on such topics as organizing, the roots of power, fundraising, or building coalitions; intensive training sessions to develop organizing strategy and tactics; classroom visits; booksigning parties; and concerts.

For more information, contact

Josh Dunson
Real People's Music
520 South Clinton Street
Oak Park, IL 60304

telephone: 708-386-1252